ONTARIO'S

Ghost Town

HERITAGE

ONTARIO'S
Ghost Town
HERITAGE

RON BROWN

The BOSTON
MILLS PRESS

Copyright © 2007 Ron Brown

First Printing

Library and Archives Canada Cataloguing in Publication
Brown, Ron, 1945-
Ontario's ghost town heritage / Ron Brown.
ISBN-13: 978-1-55046-467-2
ISBN-10: 1-55046-467-1
1. Ghost towns – Ontario – History.
2. Ghost towns – Ontario – Guidebooks.
3. Ontario – History, Local. I. Title.
FC3061.B79 2007   971.3   C2007-902034-8

Publisher Cataloging-in-Publication Data (U.S.)
Brown, Ron, 1945-
Ontario's ghost town heritage / Ron Brown.
[208] p. : col. ill., maps ;   cm.
Includes index.
Summary: An illustrated guide to the ghost towns of Ontario, including
eighty accessible locations throughout the province, with maps
and contemporary and historic photographs.
ISBN-13: 978-1-55046-467-2   (pbk.)
ISBN-10: 1-55046-467-467-1   (pbk.)
1. Ghost towns – Ontario – Guidebooks. I. Title.
917.13044 dc22   F1057.7.B769 2007

Published by Boston Mills Press, 2007
132 Main Street, Erin, Ontario N0B 1T0
Tel: 519-833-2407   Fax: 519-833-2195

In Canada:
Distributed by Firefly Books Ltd.
66 Leek Crescent, Richmond Hill, Ontario, Canada L4B 1H1

In the United States:
Distributed by Firefly Books (U.S.) Inc.
P.O. Box 1338, Ellicott Station, Buffalo, New York 14205

Design by Linda Norton-McLaren

Printed in China

*The publisher gratefully acknowledges for the financial support
of our publishing program the Canada Council, the Ontario Arts Council,
and the Government of Canada through the Book Publishing
Industry Development Program (BPIDP).*

A miner's cabin survives from the days when
Blairton led the province in iron production.

CONTENTS

Uffington's one-time Methodist
church now stands empty.

ACKNOWLEDGMENTS

Across Ontario there lies a wealth that the traveller, geographer and historian would be foolish to ignore. This treasure trove of knowledge lies within the many local history books and articles so lovingly prepared by historical societies, women's groups, municipal committees, conservation authorities, and simply by individuals who care so passionately about saving and celebrating their heritage. This information is carefully preserved in local libraries, museums and archives, and nowadays on web sites as well. Were it not for those responsible, the information in this volume would have been impossible to assemble.

I want to thank my older daughter, Jeri, for her expertise with digital images, an area where I am admittedly a novice. To my younger daughter, Ria, I am grateful for her spending much of her summer vacation editing and inputting the information for this volume. Her time in front of a computer screen while the sun shone gave me the freedom to wander the roads in search of places that are barely there. And to my wife, June, my thanks for tolerating my lengthy absences to field-check and photograph Ontario's many ghost town sites.

In these ways this book has been a collaborative effort of which I hope those I have acknowledged will approve.

A black and white view of Nicholson shows the workers' cabins and the Catholic church when the tie-mill town was thriving.

ROADS OF BROKEN DREAMS

ONTARIO'S GHOST TOWN TRAILS

This weathered house was once home
to Herron's Mills' busy sawyer.

In a province better known for its unchecked sprawl and gridlocked traffic, how, one might logically ask, can this place have "ghost towns"? Such images are surely better associated with the goldfields of British Columbia or the deserts of Arizona. But despite such misconceptions, Ontario does indeed enjoy a legacy of abandoned settlements, many more colourful or photogenic than those in better-known ghost town areas.

Ontario has passed through many phases in its recent history, phases that included military towns, tiny ports, pioneer hamlets and early mill towns. The railway era brought with it more changes in the landscape, and the places that were bypassed by the laying of the tracks fell silent. As the pioneer fringes moved northward, the exploitation of the forest and the discovery of rich deposits of gold and silver led to the boom and bust cycle that accompanied the depletion of these valuable resources.

Ontario's earliest inhabitants, our First Nations peoples, left little in the way of a ghost town legacy. By and large they were nomadic hunters and gatherers who followed the migratory patterns of their game. Even the farming tribes such as the Huron moved on after the soils they were tilling lost their fertility.

The earliest stage of development to accompany permanent European settlement was the military phase. Following the American Revolution, the emphasis of the British in Canada was decidedly upon defence. Around the many little forts across the province were small settlements known as bridgeheads, linked by military roads. Each bridgehead consisted of a military garrison and a village to supply the soldiers with skilled trades, craftsmen and farmers to supply food.

Several bridgeheads developed into larger towns, thanks to the growing use of the old military highways. Smaller bridgeheads vanished, however, when hostilities ceased and the forts were no longer needed. These in effect became Ontario's first ghost towns. Two examples are Charlotteville on the shore of Lake Erie near Turkey Point, where only a cairn marks this vanished place, and Fort Willow, a re-creation of which sits beside a swamp northwest of Barrie.

As settlement began in earnest, the government established a series of four administrative districts, each of which needed a district seat to house the governor, the court and the jail. As Ontario was further divided into more districts, and eventually into counties, new seats of government appeared and in at least two places the district seats fell vacant. One was Presqu'ile near Brighton, and another Old Johnstown east of Brockville.

With the end of the American Revolution, many Americans were forced to flee their land, often for the "crime" of remaining neutral during the upheaval. These United Empire Loyalists gave Ontario its first great pulse of settlement. Crude roads were carved into the bush and along these roads crude stopping places appeared … simple log cabins that served as way stations where travellers could eat and sleep, usually on a hard floor.

As the forests began to give way to fields of crops and pastures, crossroad hamlets clustered around road intersections. Here, pioneer farmers could barter for supplies or pick up their mail, and then settle in for a pint of their favourite beverage. These centres typically consisted of a general store, a hotel, a blacksmith shop and other craft shops. But with the inauguration of rural mail delivery and the success of the temperance movement across Ontario, many general stores and hotels shut down and many crossroads hamlets became ghost hamlets.

Meanwhile, along the lakes, any little cove that could shelter a schooner developed into a small port. Grain elevators, warehouses, and hotels provided for the business of shipping lumber, wheat and barley. But with the dawn of the steam age, and the proliferation of steamboats and, later,

Log ruins abound at the completely
abandoned mountaintop settlement
of Newfoundout.

The Keeley mine was one of Silver Centre's
more important producers. Its demise
meant the end of the community.

railways, the little coves could not compete with larger industrial harbours, and they too joined the list of ghosted settlements.

With its dense forest cover, Ontario was once traversed by countless rushing streams, and on any stream with enough flow, mills were built. The first were the sawmills that furnished settlers with the lumber to build their cabins and barns. As the new fields became productive, grist- and flourmills were added, and stores, shops and homes clustered around the mill sites.

But as the protective canopy of trees gave way to bare fields, the ground water tables lowered, depriving the smaller steams of their year-round flow. They often flooded in the spring and would dry out in the summer, with the result that the early mills could not continue. Then, with the movement of grain farming to the Canadian Prairies, the grist- and flourmills of Ontario either converted to feed mills for cattle, or closed. Many of the little towns that had relied on the mills for their existence fell silent in their turn.

The westward and northward spread of railways in the mid-1850s exacted a deadly toll on many of Ontario's fledgling villages. Communities that were ignored by the railway surveyors lost their industries to railside and often had no other reason to exist. But the railways created new towns of their own, often laid out on land owned by the railway companies themselves. Around the stations sprang up water towers, hotels, warehouses and cattle yards – all the necessary facilities to move people and goods around Ontario. With the closure of rail operation about a century after their arrival, many of these railside villages either had to adapt to the auto age, or were vacated. The latter tended more to be the case in northern Ontario where railside settlements were isolated or failed to receive road access.

By the mid-nineteenth century the farmlands of southern Ontario were filled to overflowing, and the government of the day looked northward to expand. In the

In the heyday of the Victoria Mine, the CPR railway station was a busy place.

Most of Silver Islet's "ghosts" are
now located in the graveyard of
this reviving ghost town.

area known today as "cottage country," there stood vast stands of virgin pine upon which lumber companies gazed with profit-hungry eyes. But these entrepreneurs lacked the manpower to work the lumber camps, and the farmers to provide horses and produce for those camps.

In response, the Ontario government launched its ill-fated colonization road scheme, building roads that would later be dubbed roads of broken dreams. Twenty-five in number, these rough trails wound through the rocky outcrops and dense forests between the Ottawa River and Georgian Bay. Land along the roads was free for any settler who cleared a few acres and erected a small shanty. Small villages soon followed. But once the lumber companies had ravaged the forests and moved on, the settlers discovered that the rocky soils were too infertile for self-sustaining farms. Disheartened – and often starving – the farmers fled, many of them to the west, leaving abandoned farms and roads lined with ghost hamlets in their wake.

The pines that the lumber companies harvested were at first floated downstream to sawmills at the mouths of the many rivers that flowed into Georgian Bay, making its shorelines the most industrialized in Ontario. The mill towns that grew up around these sites contained, in addition to the large and noisy (and polluting) mills, goodly numbers of hotels, stores, boarding houses and streets of simple wooden cabins. But, following a by-now common pattern, once the timber limits were depleted, the mills, most of them isolated, fell silent. The wooden structures crumbled and gradually disappeared, becoming mere mounds of rubble in new young forests.

As the railways stretched their iron ribbons into the forests of northern Ontario, another phase of settlement opened up – the era of the railside mill town. No longer dependent upon rivers for transporting timber, lumber barons simply built sawmills by the railway lines. Here, too, little towns developed, with hotels and stores lining

The main street of the mill town
of French River was laid out
along impossibly rocky terrain.

the tracks by the stations, bunkhouses for the rail crews and, in many areas, trading posts for the Cree and Ojibway to bring their furs. But again, with the depletion of the forest and the modernization of the railways, these little towns fell into disuse and their remains vanished from the tracks.

The railway also allowed eager prospectors to expand their search for the gold and silver that they believed lurked in the rocks of northern Ontario. A few of the luckier struck it rich and became millionaires. Boom towns appeared across the northland. Many were company towns built by the mining companies themselves; others were lusty boom towns that sprouted on rocky outcrops where no town should ever be built. But many of the mineral deposits were small and, as the gold or silver ran out and miners left, these habitations too joined the ranks of Ontario's ghost towns.

Ontario also experienced the growth of special towns created for specific purposes. Burwash was an isolated town near Sudbury built to house the many staff who guarded the inmates at the Burwash prison farm. Abandoned when the prison closed in the early 1970s, it was taken over by the military and removed. Another, the now-abandoned radar base of Foymount, was built atop one of Ontario's highest mountains, making it Ontario's "highest" town. Its remains still stand. Towns like Corbyville and Marlbank were built to serve specific industries, a distillery and a cement plant respectively, and their ruins remain to this day. And John Rudolphus Booth's extensive grain port of Depot Harbour, one of the Great Lakes' busiest, has left some of the most extensive ghost town ruins in the province.

How, then, does one "find" ghost towns? Fortunately, Ontarians often take a particular interest in the history of their locality, and library shelves are crammed with books and files containing accounts of local history. In the 1870s and 1880s County Atlases became popular.

An old Dalton house is on its last legs.

Log boarding houses were common
in the village that served Gold Rock's
several short-lived mines.

Created for each of Ontario's counties, these atlases showed all existing villages, complete with their buildings, owners and businesses. As these years represented the peak of country village development, these atlases still provide a glimpse of the many places that were later abandoned.

During this period business directories also came into being. These useful publications listed each village, along with a geographic description and the businesses that could be found within it. Insurance maps for company towns and old topographic maps also reveal to history buffs the layout of many towns that today no longer exist.

Defining exactly what a "ghost town" is (or should be) is not so simple. The words conjure up images of the dusty main streets and wind-blown tumbleweed of Hollywood westerns. But in reality, such places are usually found only on those movie sets. Only in rare cases have abandoned towns been preserved, because they are just that … abandoned. Val Jalbert in Quebec and Fayette in Michigan, as well as the remarkable Bodie in California, are exceptions to this rule, and not incidentally have proven to be strong tourist attractions. But for the most part, a ghost town is a place that quite simply is a "ghost" of what it once was. At its best, it would have been clearly identifiable as a town or a village and not just a scattered rural settlement. And while it may have no surviving buildings now, or may even retain a surviving handful of residents, to be a "ghost town," it would need to offer some ghostly vestige of why it was once grand … weathered buildings, mysterious foundations, or simply the remains of the old village streets.

Ontario is a vast province. The east-west drive across it takes three days, while its northern reaches remain beyond the access of the auto. Tucked away in many of its corners, beyond the 12-lane highways and past the endless rows of look-alike houses, lie the stories of prosperity and poverty that come alive on Ontario's ghost town trails, its roads of broken dreams.

An early view of Biscotasing with its first CP station. The mill sits in the background.

An early image depicts the days when Bedford Mills was an active mill town.
(The Patterson collection)

CHAPTER I

TRAILS TO THE
EAST

(not to scale)

This board and batten building served as Allisonville's
cheese factory. Its remains are now a grassy meadow.

(Library and Archives Canada)

ALLISONVILLE

The old winding stage road that linked the villages of Wellington and Rednersville in the early years of the nineteenth century has long since been straightened and paved, and is now lined with sprawling modern homes. But in the 1830s, halfway along the road, the cascading waters of Consecon Creek powered the early saw- and gristmills of Charles and William Allison, and gave rise to the village of Allisonville.

In the *Picton Gazette* of 1938, one of Allisonville's long-time residents, Mr. A.L. Calnan, recorded his early recollections of the town: "My earliest memories of Allisonville are of saw and grist mills ... the mills disappeared long ago ... Allisonville was quite a fair-sized community with several homes and the usual stores and blacksmith shops, etc." Calnan recounted fond memories of watching George Young at his blacksmithing, of the weekly entertainments at the nearby schoolhouses, and of James Boyd, postmaster and manager of the general store.

"James Boyd and his wife came to Allisonville in the early 1880s. Their store was well stocked and for many years was a popular neighbourhood gathering place. In the evening during the summer months the place was crowded." Their store remained in the Boyd family almost until 1960, its last owner being Mrs. Helen Boyd.

George Young, the blacksmith, also ran a tavern during the 1880s, although he himself was a teetotaller. The active little village could also count two asheries where wood ash was manufactured into potash. Gideon Pine, the village cooper, specialized in barrels and churns. James Robbins and Horatio Titus were other early storeowners, while Hiram Forshee, in the 1880s, ran a shingle mill. When dairying became a popular farming venture in the 1880s and 1890s, George Ferguson opened a small cheese factory.

With the arrival of the Prince Edward County Railway in the 1870s, urbanization drew industries to the growing railway towns of Picton and Wellington. Allisonville's businesses closed and most residents departed. Only the general store survived the exodus and it, too, is now a memory.

Bushes now mark the sites of the cheese factory, the blacksmith shop and the cooperage, while a number of newer homes now occupy the former farm fields. The creek runs dry for most of the year and only the outline of the old millpond remains. The Orange Hall, however, now enlarged, still stands proudly. The Wellington Lodge, located at the corner of the Dutch Road, is a handsome example of early Ontario's rural architecture and the lone reminder of a once-bustling country village.

Allisonville's Orange Lodge survives as the Wellington Lodge.

AULTSVILLE

One of Ontario's earliest water highways was the St. Lawrence River. But with its many rapids, it could only be navigated with the use of locks and portages. Several villages grew around the locks and at various landings along the route.

Then, on the July 1, 1958, the floodgates of the St. Lawrence Seaway were opened and the waters raced over the remains of these one-time riverside communities. Milles Roche, Farran's Point, Dickinson's Landing, Wales and Aultsville all disappeared beneath the river currents.

Many buildings from the doomed communities had been moved to the new towns of Ingleside and Long Sault, or to the historical park at Upper Canada Village. Most, however, were simply demolished. While almost all the abandoned village sites now lie well below the canal's waters, those of Aultsville still lie near the surface, leaving some of the sidewalks and old backyards exposed.

Aultsville's origins date to the day when Richard Loucks, a United Empire Loyalist refugee, opened a tavern on his 400-acre farm in 1792. For several years, court sessions for the newly formed district of Lunenburg took place in Loucks' tavern. Travel was by the military road that hugged the banks of the swirling St. Lawrence River. As more settlers arrived to take up land, a settlement grew around the tavern and became known as Charlesville. With the beginning of the Richelieu and Ontario Navigation Company, steamers began to call, and a town plan was laid out with street names like Melburn, York, Nelson and Palace. Tan Bark Avenue led to Thomas Brown's tannery. During the 1840s the newly opened post office adopted the name Aultsville after another founding Loyalist family, the Aults.

In 1856 the Grand Trunk Railway opened its Aultsville station, and river traffic dwindled. With the arrival of the trains, the town grew to include, in addition to the tannery, four shoemakers, a sawmill, a shingle mill and two brickyards. The Riverview Hotel replaced the old Loucks Tavern, but following a plebiscite in 1903 was prohibited from serving liquor. The presence of three churches, United, Anglican and Presbyterian, may have had something to do with the success of the "dry" vote. Residents could also enjoy a riverside memorial park or send their children to the local school.

With the arrival of the auto age after the Second World War, Aultsville's industries and businesses began to move or to close. By the mid-1950s, only Borden's Chateau cheese factory and the Jarvis and Shaver general store remained.

Aultsville lies south of the former Highway 2, a short distance east of Upper Canada Village and on the park road (formerly the Aultsville Road), which leads to Morrison and Nairn islands. While the road bends left, the pavement of the former Aultsville Road continues straight ahead.

Where the pavement ends and a causeway over a man-made swamp begins, look in the bushes for the sidewalks, lanes and overgrown yards that once belonged to a thriving riverside town. Aultsville's Grand Trunk Station was relocated to a small roadside park 2 km (1.2 miles) west of the entrance to Upper Canada Village.

FRATERNITY HALL.
PUBLIC SCHOOL.
AULTSVILLE. ONT.

A grainy postcard image is all that is left of this drowned village's former main street, which now lies beneath the St. Lawrence Seaway.

Only vague evidence of the village's roads and sidewalks remains above the flooded St. Lawrence Seaway.

Balaclava's abandoned general store hides
behind a growth of shrubs.

Right: Balaclava's old mill still dominates
the ghost main street.

BALACLAVA
(Renfrew County)

ocated on a settlement road that linked the Opeongo Road with the town of Douglas, Balaclava developed as a mill town on Constant Creek in 1855. In 1868 the mill was acquired by the Richards family and it would go on to operate for nearly a century.

By 1860 the town had added a blacksmith shop and hotel, and several small houses lined the road in both directions. By 1903 so much sawdust was clogging the stream that a downstream gristmill, using newly passed federal anti-pollution legislation, took the Richardses to court and won. Shortly thereafter the Richardses added a sawdust burner. In 1936 much of the original mill was destroyed in a fire. Wood from a neighbouring sawmill was used to reconstruct the mill. When cutting at full capacity, the mill was capable of producing a million board feet of lumber per week.

But few railways made their way into the rugged highlands of Renfrew County, and Balaclava was one of many communities that were bypassed by these new lifelines. The little village continued doggedly to rely on the production of the water-powered mill for its survival.

However, by 1957 the surrounding timber supply had run out and the mill could produce little more than a few thousand board feet per year. Production continued to dwindle and after a few more years the mill fell silent and the store closed. The hotel and blacksmith had already given up many years earlier. The hotel burned down in the early 1990s, and the site is now overgrown with weeds.

The former blacksmith shop and the large store, both vacant, still stand beside each other, picturesquely weathered, although in the summer a healthy growth of bushes obscures the facades. However, across the road from the old mill pond, beside the rushing river, still looms the huge form of the sawmill, burner and all.

The site lies on Scotch Bush Road (formerly Highway 513), 3 km (1.8 miles) north of the hamlet of Dacre, which is on Highway 132.

Bedford Mills' main street passes between the power house and the mill.

An early image depicts the days when Bedford Mills was an active mill town. *(The Patterson collection)*

BEDFORD MILLS

Set against a backdrop of forests and cliffs, this little ghost hamlet of Bedford Mills, with the foaming Buttermilk Falls beside it, draws photographers and backroad ramblers alike to its picturesque setting. The stone mill building reflects in a pond, a backwater that formerly linked the community with the Rideau Canal.

When the canal was completed in 1832, Benjamin Tett entered into a partnership with another family of entrepreneurs, the Chaffeys, who erected saw- and gristmills beside the waterfalls. Tett took sole ownership in 1834 and added a boarding house and several cabins for his workers. In 1847 he replaced his early sawmill and added the stone gristmill that survives to this day.

When the railway era wrought economic hardship on the canal, Tett's sons diversified and added to Bedford Mills' activities a cheese factory, mica mining and barge building. The mine lasted only a few years, closing in 1908.

At its peak, Bedford Mills, with its mills, church, school, powerhouse and homes large and small, contained more than 150 residents. In the "lower" town by the millponds were the store, the school and St. Stephen's Anglican Church, as well as the mill and a new powerhouse, which used the power from the waterfall. Atop the granite ridge stood the "upper" town with a boarding house, private dwellings and the sawmill.

But canal traffic continued to decline and the railway lines went elsewhere. The mica mines were depleted and farmers moved away from the rocky soil. In 1916 the mill ceased operation and Bedford Mills fell silent. However, cottaging and retirement living have restored part of it to life. Some of its stately homes have become summer residences, while the handsome white frame St. Stephen's Church still sees occasional worship.

The powerhouse beside the foaming falls has been converted to a workshop, and the mill into a private home. Along the road and on the rocky ridge, the young forest has grown over foundations and streets that have been silent for half a century.

To reach Bedford Mills, follow the Perth Road (County Road 10) north from Kingston or south from Westport to the "Bedford Mills Road." The ghost mill village lurks only a short distance away.

Bedford Mills' old mill reflects picturesquely in the millpond.

BLAIRTON

Iron was one of Ontario's earliest mineral products, and Blairton was one of the province's first iron producers. Until the 1840s much of Ontario's iron came from bog ore, extracted from peat and heated by wood. During this era, a small village on the shore of Lake Erie, named Normandale, produced most of the output. But once the bog ore had been depleted, iron producers like Joseph Van Norman (after whom Normandale was named) sought out ore in the bedrock.

The "big ore bed" was discovered on the shores of Crowe Lake, then a remote lake near present-day Marmora. However, in the Ontario of the 1850s and 1860s, roads were almost impassable, and the cost of shipping the ore was prohibitive. In 1866 the newly formed Cobourg & Peterborough Railway provided an economical way to ship ore, and the village of Blairton was laid out at the mine site.

A contemporary writer has noted: "The mine reopened in 1867, employing 300 miners, and the quiet little village of Blairton became a bustling community." Here, on a grid network of a dozen streets, stood 40 cabins, a school, the Wesleyan church, and the Orange Hall, along with three general stores, two boarding houses, three hotels (including the well-frequented Purdy House) and various other businesses. The railway itself had a small station and engine house.

The company prepared for a surge of miners by surveying a town with 11 streets and 220 lots. Most were quickly purchased. The busy corner of King and Queen streets witnessed a constant coming and going of shoppers and hotel patrons, while some distance away, beyond the boarding houses on John St., rose the din and the dust of the ironworks. But even more miners were needed; the Province of Ontario gazetteer for 1869 exclaimed: "Even though the land is almost all taken up, miners and labourers are in great demand."

By 1870 Blairton's population had topped 500, and it was the largest community in the area. But shipping continued to be expensive, as it required barges as well as rail. In 1875, when water inundated the pit, operations ended.

The arrival of the Ontario & Quebec Railway in 1884 renewed hopes that shipping would become cheaper, but the mine never revived. By 1900 only two dozen people remained in the desolate townsite. Despite its age, Blairton has managed to retain old buildings, foundations and streets that recall, if only vaguely, its heyday.

About 7 km (4.2 miles) west of Marmora, Blairton Road leads north of Highway 7 about 2 km (1.2 miles) to the town site. At the first intersection of the old village roads, King and Queen, is the site of the former store. Between Queen and Cole Road, newer homes mingle with mine-era cabins. Opposite them, on the east side of Blairton Road, are the cellar holes of the hotels and shops that once made Blairton a bustling town.

The dog-leg on Cole Road west of Blairton Road reflects the former grid pattern of the old town plot and leads to the only surviving two-storey company house, now used as a storage shed, and just beyond that another of the miners' tiny cabins.

Following Blairton's demise, Marmora became the focus of local iron making, a heritage that is celebrated with an historic plaque and preserved ruins in the village's pretty riverside park.

Of many company houses built for
Blairton's miners, only one survives.

BRUDENELL

By the 1850s most of the timber and farmland in southern Ontario was gone. To the north, in today's "cottage country" lay vast hillsides of tall pine timber stands. Despite the yearnings of the lumber companies, there were no farms, workers, horses or roads to cut and ship the fallen timber. To open up the forested highlands between the Ottawa River Valley and Georgian Bay, the government devised its "colonization road" scheme.

Overtly, it was touted as a philanthropic initiative to provide settlers with free land and to ease crowded farmlands in southern Ontario. In reality the plan was little more than a means of providing Ontario's influential lumber companies with the labour, food and horses they needed, while the land proved to be largely rock and swamp.

For as long as lumbering continued, the colonization road settlements prospered. Soon, however, the lumber companies had clear-cut the magnificent pine stands, bringing the end of markets and jobs for the settlers. Unable to create economical farms on the harsh land, most of the colonizers fled, lured by the promise of better lands on Canada's prairies. Behind them lay the abandoned farms and the ghost towns on their roads of broken dreams.

The junction of colonization roads almost invariably spawned strategically placed villages. By 1871 the Opeongo Road was lined with a string of busy hotels, and at its intersection with another key route, the Peterson Road (known first as Brudenell Corners), three hotels were in full operation. Their owners, James Grace, James Whelan and Mme Desirée Payette, included taverns to quench the thirsts of the boisterous lumbermen.

The permanent settlers of the Opeongo Road also required services, and the busy intersection soon boasted three general stores, two blacksmiths, shoemakers and carpenters, as well as a church, a hall and a school in addition to its population of almost two hundred. Brudenell also enjoyed a daily stage service to Combermere and Rockingham, southwest on the Peterson Road, and to Eganville to the northeast. With the construction of the J.R. Booth's Canada Atlantic Railway in 1893, the railway station at Killaloe, some 16 km (10 miles) north, became the new stage destination.

By 1885 James Costello was operating one of the general stores, and Mike Costello opened a blacksmith shop and purchased one of the hotels. Meanwhile Mme Payette had purchased John Devine's hotel (originally Whelan's) for a sum of $2,000, while Devine busied himself with the construction of settlement roads.

In 1893 the extension of Booth's railway took business away from the Opeongo Road villages and they diminished in importance, Brudenell among them. Only the Costellos remained with the hotel, store and blacksmith shop.

Today most of the Opeongo Road has been paved and now forms a section of Highway 512. While a few of Brudenell's original buildings, including the old hotel and store, still stand at the intersection, none have retained their original function, and sit vacant or are used only as seasonal residences. A short distance east, the former school is now a home, while 2 km (1.2 miles) west, the stone Catholic church continues in use.

A lonely store still stands on the main street of Brudenell.

Brudenell's former hotel and store lend a ghostly air to the Opeongo Road.

Top: Corbyville's main street consists mainly of former company buildings, including the stone store.

The government excise bonding warehouses are vacant now even though the grass remains neatly trimmed.

CORBYVILLE

In 1857 Henry Corby arrived on the shores of the Moira River north of Belleville and established a grist mill along with a distillery to handle the poorer quality grain. Soon his distillery became the largest in the county and proved more profitable than his grist operation. Corby then began to dabble in politics, becoming first the mayor of nearby Belleville and later a member of the provincial legislature for the Liberals. In 1881 his son Harry assumed operations, selling whisky by the bottle rather than by the barrel. Prohibition in the U.S during the 1920s brought a boom in production, and the town was expanded to include new vats as well as company offices, customs sheds and a small company townsite. A 1928 insurance map shows about three dozen buildings covering the site, including a general store and eight semi-detached houses.

About this time, Corby's merged with Wiser's Distillery and adopted the name Canadian Industrial Alcohol Company. By 1950, however, it had taken back its old name; as the H. Corby Distillery Company, it continued to grow and expand. Although Corbyville provided housing for its workers, the polluted air forced many to choose nearby Cannifton or Belleville for their homes.

Finally, in 1991, the plant closed and 180 workers needed to find new jobs and homes. The company houses were dismantled, as were a number of the plant buildings. Most of the remaining structures, however, have survived, giving the appearance of an abandoned main street. Among them are the original stone bottling plant, which was later shown on the plan as the store, the former pump house (1910) and the stables across the road from it. Attached to the bottling plant are the former company offices and administrative buildings, more recently occupied by the Thurlow Township municipal offices. Opposite this row of buildings are the Canadian Government excise bonding warehouses, which are now closed, although their small yards remain neatly trimmed.

The now-vacant sites of the eight company houses and the vats are weedy and litter-strewn, with only a former vat house still in place. Across the field and separate from the townsite lie a grouping of tankhouses that date from 1918–20. At the south end of the main street, the River Inn banquet hall, a relatively new building dating from 1979, and the garden and fountain beside it, preserve the attractive entrance to the company townsite.

Adjacent to the River Inn stands the former 1920 fire hall, now home to the Moira River Kayak and Canoe Club. An old sidewalk wobbles its way from the fire hall to a small row of surviving workers' houses. At the north end of the site the manager's house, a large and attractive stone building remains a private residence.

Located on the northern fringe of the growing city of Belleville, the Official Plan for the area designates Corbyville as an historic village which, while permitting new housing, stores and industrial plants, also proposes to preserve the historic structures that line the ghost main street. Corbyville lies along Cannifton Road a short distance past Short Road.

CRAIGMONT

Once the world's largest producer of corundum, the ghost town of Craigmont now sleeps in the shadow of Mt. Robillard. In 1876 an early settler named Henry Robillard, while picking berries with his daughter, noticed rocks that resembled, the girl thought, cruet stoppers. Twenty years would pass though before these "stoppers" were finally identified as corundum, then considered the hardest known mineral (second to the more elusive and expensive diamonds). In 1900 the Canada Corundum Company leased 1,400 acres (0.4 ha) on the mountain and converted an existing sawmill into a crusher.

Named for its first vice-president, B.B. Craig, Craigmont, with its population of 400, consisted of both a company town and a private town. The eastern portion was the company town with offices, boarding houses, and workers' cabins. The private town developed a short distance to the west, with the school, church, private businesses and houses that were more substantial in size. Craigmont also enjoyed the luxury of telephone service and a visiting surgeon from St. Michael's Hospital in Toronto. Stage service linked Craigmont with the sawmill town and port of Combermere on Lake Kaminiskeg, a short distance north.

The only thing missing was a tavern, for Ontario law prohibited alcohol in mining towns. Thirsty workers were forced to hike the 8 km (5 miles) into the port of Combermere. By 1904 there were 200 miners at work in the mines and the mill; by two years later this had doubled to 400. Because most of the local populace could at best supply only seasonal labour, the company was forced to rely on labourers imported from Europe. As mine manager, H.E. Haultein, reported: "The local labour supply is small and very irregular, depending upon the seasons and the harvest, and the supply is kept up by importation, not quite so systematic or so coercive as the Transvaal but still containing all the unsatisfactory elements of labour importation."

A larger crusher soon replaced the converted sawmill and was producing 80 per cent of Canada's corundum needs. From high on Mt. Robillard, the echo of explosions signalled the start of the crushing and milling process. Each blast would liberate 3,000–4,000 tons of ore. Stoneboats dragged the crushed rock to a tramway, which in turn carried the ore into the upper portion of the mill. A wet separation process forced the heavier corundum to separate from the lighter material. The corundum then would travel over rollers to the drying room, where mill workers waited to hand-separate it into 18 different sizes and pack it into 100 lb (450 gram) bags. Following this operation, a tramway would again transport the bags to barges waiting at a landing on the nearby York River. The next stop was the railway at Barry's Bay at the north end of Kaminiskeg Lake, from where the corundum made its way to market.

Then, in 1913, the mill burned to the ground, and production was shifted to another crusher at the nearby Burgess mine. By 1921 all activity had ceased and Craigmont became a ghost town.

Nevertheless, Craigmont comes alive during summer months when rockhounds from across the continent comb the hillsides of Mt. Robillard, scratching for crystals of the mineral that gave Craigmont its reason to exist, corundum.

Craigmont is located 2–3 km (1.5–2 miles) along Craigmont Road, which leads east from Highway 517 about 8 km (5 miles) south of Combermere. (Avoid the temptation to use "Craigmont Road" leading out of the village of Combermere itself. After reaching a small cluster of houses, it becomes impassable for most vehicles.) Although the better access road is difficult for passenger vehicles, it is passable in dry weather. Where the road forks right, a solitary log cabin stands in an overgrown meadow. It remains occupied. The left fork leads to the site of the smelter, now reduced to scattered foundations in the bush on the west side of the road. A seasonal cabin on the east side of the road and rough clearings with vague cellar holes further along were also part of the long-vanished town.

Most of the former townsite today lies on privately owned land.

One of Craigmont's few remaining cabins now sports a rooftop solar panel.

The ruins of the Craigmont refinery lie well hidden by brush.

Trains of the Central Ontario Railway called regularly during Eldorado's more prosperous period.

John St. with its early buildings leads to the site of the now-vanished station and the railway roadbed.

ELDORADO

North of Madoc on Highway 62, the village of Eldorado is quiet now. A few old frame buildings, weathered and worn, stand beside potholed streets. Yet the village's name evokes a once-promising destiny – a destiny that within an astonishingly short time would falter and fail.

When the word "gold" echoed from what was then the wilderness of northern Hastings County in 1866, a settlement of hotels, bars, brothels and outfitters appeared overnight and took the name Eldorado, city of gold. Nuggets of gold "the size of butternuts" beckoned prospectors and speculators from across Canada. They crowded onto stages and private wagons, or walked from the port of Belleville to the hastily constructed boom town at the end of the road.

Within weeks, Eldorado was a bustling town of more than 80 buildings. A town plan was quickly drawn up with a grid of streets named John, Richardson, and Charles lying west of the Hastings Road. "Upper" Eldorado stood atop a lofty granite ridge, while "lower" Eldorado occupied the flats below. As the place bulged with restless miners and prospectors, a hastily assembled squad of mounted police set up a base in nearby Madoc.

When whispers spread that the original claim was a fake, a mob of miners led by the veteran of the Cariboo gold rush, "Cariboo" Cameron, descended on the hapless mine manager. Two of the mob were allowed in to see the prospects and emerged bursting with enthusiasm. (It was later speculated that they were paid off to make the false claims so that the land value of the mine would rise.) The mounties rushed from their quarters in Madoc but arrived only after the vigilantes had retired to one of the local waterholes to drink to their good fortune. While there were several establishments in which to imbibe, the most popular were the Anglo Hotel, the North American Hotel, the Royal Hotel and the Wannamaeker Boarding House, a portion of which still stands.

Many of the gold claims proved to be impossible to mill, or, as feared, simply fraudulent. Most of the prospectors shuffled gloomily home and Eldorado fell silent. In the 1890s new processing techniques allowed some mines to re-open. The arrival of the Central Ontario Railway in 1884 meant that local farmers could ship out milk and lumber from the tiny Eldorado station. Around this time the town also gained new life with a box factory, a cheese factory and a short-lived talc mine and copper refinery.

But the mines, too, were short-lived and have long since ceased operation. The rails have been lifted and Eldorado has become a near ghost town, its 80 buildings now reduced to two dozen. Many of them started as hotels but no longer serve that use. Streets once lined with homes are now private lanes. The site of the train station is marked only by the concrete platform, while the roadbed has become a snowmobile trail.

The story of Eldorado and the Hastings gold rush is retold on an historic plaque at the corner of Highway 62 and John St., beside a brick building that was the Wannamaeker Boarding House. On the east side of the Hastings Road stand the former Strebe's general store, now ghostly and weathered; and a short distance south, now a convenience store, is the former Pigden gas station and car dealership.

Meanwhile. in the hills above the town, the crumbling ruins of the Richardson crusher and the site of Ontario's first gold mine lie forgotten by all but the town's few remaining residents.

The ghosts of Eldorado straddle Highway 62 about 12 km (7.5 miles) north of Madoc. (Note: a cheese factory a short distance south still uses the name "Eldorado Gold" on its products.)

FLEETWOOD

Nestled in the rolling hills between Lake Scugog and Rice Lake, Fleetwood was first settled by Irish immigrants and named after a village in their homeland.

These early settlers followed ancient Indian trails from Port Darlington and Port Whitby on Lake Ontario. Here, on the 11th Concession of Manvers Township, one of the founding families, the Staples, laid out a townsite with such street names as Queen, Mill and Mount Fall. To supply much-needed lumber to the new arrivals, two sawmills were built which operated until the 1890s. The streets were also lined with stores belonging to James Morrow and William Stacey, as well as a shoemaker and two blacksmiths. In addition to the "Grandy Tavern," the hamlet could also claim a Methodist church and a schoolhouse.

In the 1870s the Midland Railway (later incorporated into the Grand Trunk) bypassed Fleetwood to the east. Later, in 1910, when the CPR brought in a rival branch line between its main line at Dranoel and Lindsay, it built a "Fleetwood" station, but again it stood some distance to the east and was too late to have much impact on the village's growth. Although the station consisted only of a small flag shelter, a considerable amount of livestock and wood was shipped from the busy siding.

With the rising popularity of automobiles and the accompanying road improvements, and with the death of many branch lines, the station closed. Larger towns attracted local shoppers and Fleetwood became a forgotten backwater. Although the mills had burned in the 1880s, the store lasted until 1935 and the church until 1947. The school closed a few years after that.

Most of the early structures are now gone. The schoolhouse has become a private home. Only two dwellings and a shed constitute the "downtown" of the once-busy village; one of the buildings may have been a hotel. On the hilltop to the west, the former store has become a residence. Vacant and overgrown lots mark the sites of other early homes and shops.

Private driveways both north and south of the "main street" reflect the layout of the village plan. At the east end of the "village," Old Mill Road leads to the now-overgrown mill site. Farther to the east, the former railway right of way crosses the road and is still clearly evident. The track was lifted in the 1980s and no evidence remains of the siding or the flag station.

The former schoolhouse lies 2 km (1.2 miles) west at the intersection of Fleetwood Road and St. Mary's Road, a short distance east of Highway 35. The rest of the vanished village is 2 km (1.2 miles) east of that point.

Little survives of Fleetwood's once-
busy main thoroughfare.

FOYMOUNT

One of Ontario's most historic pioneer trails, the Opeongo Colonization Road, still retains many of its heritage structures; log barns, snake rail fences, and pioneer log cabins appear frequently on this winding road. From its highest point, the view extends across the wide Ottawa Valley to the high hazy Gatineau Hills of Quebec. This made the location ideal for a town of a particular nature.

Here, atop the highest point of land in eastern Ontario, the Royal Canadian Air Force constructed a NORAD radar base. Part of the system known as the Pinetree Line, it was established to detect planes swooping down upon the United States from her "enemies" to the north. The base opened in 1950.

Named after a pioneer settlement, Foymount was a self-contained town with 65 houses, six apartment buildings, a school, a clinic, a community centre, a library, a swimming pool, and a store and post office. Water was pumped from a nearby lake, while sewage was treated on site. Its strategic hilltop location, 550 metres (1,800 feet) high, was topped with a pair of white radar domes to detect incoming enemy missiles or fighters.

During its first and busiest years, when the Cold War was in full swing, Foymount could count nearly 400 civilian and military residents, making the village Ontario's highest populated place. Subsequent changes in technology reduced the need for many of the base's functions.

Finally, as fears arising from the Cold War abated, military unification and downsizing closed the Foymount base, and in 1974 the domes were dismantled. The rest of the site was sold privately, only to be taken over later by the local municipality for outstanding taxes. Today most of the homes have new occupants, many of whom are former base personnel. The apartment blocks remain empty, however, and the sidewalks and parking lots are cracked and weed-strewn. While many of the military buildings are also empty, others have new occupants, including a clothing manufacturer and a tea room. The other buildings that remain vacant give ample gawking material for the ghost-towner.

Foymount is located about one kilometre (half a mile) west of the intersection of the Opeongo Road with Highway 512, 25 km (15 miles) west of Eganville.

While much of Foymount has revived, these vacant apartment buildings lend a decidedly ghostly air to this mountaintop radar village.

The radar domes of Ontario's highest
town, the military town of Foymount,
were removed in the 1970s.

A monument atop the steps to Glanmire's vanished St. Margaret's Church symbolizes the building's history.

GLANMIRE

At the junction of the Hastings Colonization Road with Glanmire Lake Road, an aging concrete bridge spans the turbulent Beaver Creek. About a kilometre (half a mile) farther on, at the steps of a now-vanished church, the passable portion of the Hastings Road ends. But in the days when the road was the area's major highway, a busy little village stood near the steps.

The Hastings Road was another of the government's colonization roads, opened in 1856 to lure settlers with offers of free land, settlers who were actually needed to supply the influential lumber companies with labour, produce and horses to work the remote lumber camps.

First known as Jelly's Rapids, after pioneer settler Andrew Jelly, Glanmire began as a stopping place, a bone-jarring half-day's journey north of Millbridge. Around the site there clustered a hotel, a school, a post office, a few simple frame and log dwellings, and, according to local accounts, a mill on the creek, as well as St. Margaret's Anglican Church. When the post office opened, the new name "Glanmire" was adopted.

But Glanmire's prosperity was short-lived. The Central Ontario Railway bypassed the site, and once the tall pines were gone, the lumber camps closed, leaving the once-hopeful settlers to face stony and infertile fields. A brief flurry of gold-mining activity around the turn of the century failed to revitalize the area.

Today, improbably, the steps to the site of St, Margaret's Church stand amid the headstones of a carefully kept graveyard, where many of the stones mark the burial plots of the Birrell and Lumniss families. After the church was removed in 1957, a cairn was placed atop the concrete steps to commemorate the history of the little pioneer place of worship. Where the school once stood on the adjacent lot, only foundations remain. Opposite the church and along the road, a few vague clearings constitute the only other remains of this early village.

Glanmire's concrete bridge, located near the site of the mills, belies the nearly impassable nature of the Hastings Road beyond it.

The mills at Herron's Mills have collapsed into a pile of lumber.

The bridge over the Clyde River, which once linked the various mill buildings, is in ruins.

HERRON'S MILLS

Picturesquely perched on the banks of eastern Ontario's Clyde River, Herron's Mills has been the site of milling operations since 1842 when John Gillies, a local lumber baron, built at this waterpower location a sawmill, a gristmill, an oat mill and a carding mill. Known originally as Gillies' Mills, the village grew to include a school and a store as well.

In 1861, with lumber cut from his own mill, Gillies built a large frame house that stands to this day. A decade later, in order to spend more time on his timber limits on the Clyde and Mississippi rivers, Gillies sold his house and gristmill to John Herron. Herron expanded the operation, adding a tannery, a shingle mill and accommodation for the 20-man work force.

The Herron brothers, John and James, Scottish immigrants, foresaw a bright future for the mill and the growing community. More sociable than the quieter Gillies clan, the Herrons hosted frequent skating parties on the millpond, accompanied by a bonfire and hot chocolate. They offered room and board for the teacher at the Herron Mills school. Following a damaging flood in 1896, the Herrons rebuilt the mill, even expanding its capacity. In 1891 the Herrons opened a post office, giving the growing village the name Herron's Mills. It operated out of the family home until 1915. The sawmill, when in full swing, could turn out 8,000 board feet of lumber a day. By then the original buildings had been replaced and the machinery updated. Attached to the sawmill was the gristmill with rollers, hoppers and purifying screens, while the sawmill contained more modern machinery. Although most of the mills' operations ended in the early 1940s, the J. and J. Herron Company operated sporadically until 1950.

Sadly, the mill has now collapsed into a pile of lumber on the little trail that was once the mill road. The remains of the early bridge can be seen from the bridge on the new road, marking the original route from the mill to the Gillies house. Throughout the property many ruins and vacant structures still stand in overgrown fields. An abandoned house, said to have belonged to the sawyer, stands at the intersection of Highway 511. The historic Gillies home, now renovated, remains one of the area's key heritage homes. Sadly, plans to preserve the complex within a conservation area were not successful. Although the property remains private, most of the remnants, as well as the Gillies house, can be easily viewed from the roadside.

The ghosts of Herron's Mills lie about 4 km (2.5 miles) north of the village of Lanark on Herron's Mills Road a few steps east of Highway 511. The historic house stands on the south side of the road, on the east bank of the river. The mill ruins are on the west.

LEMIEUX

Unlike many of the Ontario communities that became ghost towns, Lemieux did not fall victim to resource depletion, or economic hard times. It was abandoned because of the danger that lurked beneath its streets.

Originally, Lemieux was little more than a rural village to serve the surrounding population of French-Canadian farmers and a lumber camp. Its first postmaster was Louis Lemieux, who also operated the area's first lumber camp. The place grew to a population of about 100, with a store and a fine stone Catholic church, all of which stretched along a single dirt street.

But in 1971 a collapse of land near Jonquière in Quebec, following a prolonged rain, took more than 30 lives and sent geologists scrambling to see whether similar soil conditions threatened life elsewhere. There, beneath the houses of Lemieux, lay the deadly substratum.

Known as Lida Clay, it is a layer of fine clay particles that are rock-hard when dry, but when saturated, lose their cohesion and turn into quicksand – sucking down everything with them. New properties were purchased, families relocated and buildings demolished.

By 1990 Lemieux was a ghost town.

Then, as if on cue, an area of pastureland on the outskirts of the village collapsed during a heavy and prolonged rain, carrying into the South Nation River an area of land equal to seven football fields. Sensing the impending peril, the cattle that had been grazing the grass moments earlier had fled and were saved. A less fortunate truck driver managed to crawl away but his vehicle remained in the quagmire. The pit where the cave-in occurred has since been replanted and is now scarcely visible.

In nearby Lemieux, the sidewalks, now overgrown, still line one side of the road, while next to them shrubs and young trees hide the foundations and the driveways of the silent village. In the centre of what was once the town, former residents have returned to erect a plaque that commemorates the history and the fate of the place with the deadly dirt.

The sidewalks and plaque in Lemieux can be found 8 km (5 miles) north of Highway 417 at exit 58 on County Road 8. The site of the latest landslip is about 2 km (1.2 miles) beyond the plaque.

The road to Lemieux came to an abrupt end at the site of the massive land slip.

Only a sidewalk and a cairn survive to tell of the existence of the village that lay above the deadly dirt.

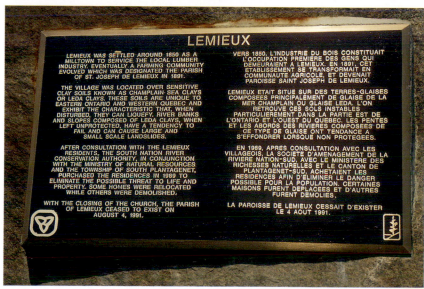

LEMIEUX

LEMIEUX WAS SETTLED AROUND 1850 AS A MILLTOWN TO SERVICE THE LOCAL LUMBER INDUSTRY. EVENTUALLY A FARMING COMMUNITY EVOLVED WHICH WAS DESIGNATED THE PARISH OF ST. JOSEPH DE LEMIEUX IN 1891.

THE VILLAGE WAS LOCATED OVER SENSITIVE CLAY SOILS KNOWN AS CHAMPLAIN SEA CLAYS OR LEDA CLAYS. THESE SOILS ARE UNIQUE TO EASTERN ONTARIO AND WESTERN QUEBEC AND EXHIBIT THE CHARACTERISTIC THAT, WHEN DISTURBED, THEY CAN LIQUEFY. RIVER BANKS AND SLOPES COMPOSED OF LEDA CLAYS, WHEN LEFT UNPROTECTED, HAVE A TENDENCY TO FAIL AND CAN CAUSE LARGE AND SMALL SCALE LANDSLIDES.

AFTER CONSULTATION WITH THE LEMIEUX RESIDENTS, THE SOUTH NATION RIVER CONSERVATION AUTHORITY, IN CONJUNCTION WITH THE MINISTRY OF NATURAL RESOURCES AND THE TOWNSHIP OF SOUTH PLANTAGENET, PURCHASED THE RESIDENCES IN 1989 TO ELIMINATE THE POSSIBLE THREAT TO LIFE AND PROPERTY. SOME HOMES WERE RELOCATED WHILE OTHERS WERE DEMOLISHED.

WITH THE CLOSING OF THE CHURCH, THE PARISH OF LEMIEUX CEASED TO EXIST ON AUGUST 4, 1991.

VERS 1850, L'INDUSTRIE DU BOIS CONSTITUAIT L'OCCUPATION PREMIERE DES GENS QUI DEMEURAIENT A LEMIEUX. EN 1891, CET ETABLISSEMENT SE TRANSFORMAIT EN COMMUNAUTE AGRICOLE, ET DEVENAIT PAROISSE SAINT JOSEPH DE LEMIEUX.

LEMIEUX ETAIT SITUE SUR DES TERRES-GLAISES COMPOSEES PRINCIPALEMENT DE GLAISE DE LA MER CHAMPLAIN OU GLAISE LEDA. L'ON RETROUVE CES SOLS INSTABLES PARTICULIEREMENT DANS LA PARTIE EST DE L'ONTARIO ET L'OUEST DU QUEBEC. LES PENTES ET LES ABORDS DES RIVIERES COMPOSEES DE CE TYPE DE GLAISE ONT TENDANCE A S'EFFONDRER LORSQUE NON PROTEGEES.

EN 1989, APRES CONSULTATION AVEC LES VILLAGEOIS, LA SOCIETE D'AMENAGEMENT DE LA RIVIERE NATION-SUD, AVEC LE MINISTERE DES RICHESSES NATURELLES ET LE CANTON DE PLANTAGENET-SUD, ACHETAIENT LES RESIDENCES AFIN D'ELIMINER LE DANGER POSSIBLE POUR LA POPULATION. CERTAINES MAISONS FURENT DEPLACEES ET D'AUTRES FURENT DEMOLIES.

LA PAROISSE DE LEMIEUX CESSAIT D'EXISTER LE 4 AOUT 1991.

The area covered by Marlbank's sprawling cement operation has now been reclaimed by forest.

MARLBANK

Not to be confused with today's village of Marlbank, the company town of that name was created in 1892, when the Rathbun Lumber Company built a cement plant and workers' village by the shore of Dry Lake, 55 km (35 miles) northeast of Belleville. Up until this time, cement was being manufactured at Napanee Mills near Napanee using an older technique that involved extracting natural cement from limestone. But a newer process, known as the "Portland" style of cement making, using marl and clay, was replacing the earlier one, and older plants had to change or be closed.

Production began in 1889, when the Rathbun Company of Deseronto extended its Bay of Quinte Railway from Tamworth to Tweed, thereby accessing the marl beds of Dry Lake. Here they built their Portland cement plant.

The Marlbank plant became highly profitable and was expanded in 1903 simply to keep up with demand. In addition to the cement plant, the Rathbun Company added boarding houses that could sleep the 100 workers, and a string of 40 employee houses. East of the cement operation by about 2 km (1.2 miles) stood the Bay of Quinte railway station, where the town of Marlbank itself prospered with several hundred residents.

By 1909 the newly formed Canada Portland Cement Company had bought control over most of Canada's cement industry, merging some plants and closing others. The plant at Marlbank was one of the victims.

Since then the site has sat silent, engulfed by a young forest. Walls have crumbled from the cement plant, and the houses have been reduced to their foundations. In the woods the plentiful ruins include stone walls, silos and rubble. From the muddy lake there occasionally emerges (depending on the water level) the hulk of a submerged saddleback steam engine that had run off its tracks and into the water.

To the east, the village of Marlbank continues to bustle, drawing upon cottagers and the area's rural population for its livelihood. Here too, the former Bay of Quinte railway station still stands, little altered and used now as a house.

The ruins in the woods lie on the south side of County Road 13 about 2 km (1.2 miles) west of Marlbank. Many of the employee houses stood on the north side of the road.

The remains of the cement workers' village and the cement plant are overwhelmed by the forest.

53

Hogan's Hotel, now a house, offered overnight accommodation to rail passengers at the site of Millbridge Station.

The East End store was busy during the days when the Hastings Road was the area's only thoroughfare.

MILLBRIDGE

A mere 60 years had passed between the days when hopeful settlers swarmed up the Hastings Colonization Road to their free grants of land and 1925, when a retired provincial land surveyor named C.F. Aylesworth looked upon the road's fate: "The mute evidence of it all is empty, dilapidated and abandoned houses, barns, orchards, wells, old broken down fences, root cellars and many other similar evidences of having given up the ghost."

"When first settled," Aylesworth went on, "there were many hotels and stopping places along this road, perhaps at intervals of every five or six miles. Now it is only the oldtimer who can point out where they stood." While places like Glanmire, Thanet, Murphy's Corner, Ormsby and Umfraville were little more than stopping places, Millbridge, with its waterpower advantage, grew into a mill town as well.

First settled by Captain Ralph Norman, a Crimean War veteran, Millbridge was originally known as the Jordan due to the waterpower advantage it enjoyed on the Jordan River. It soon acquired three hotels, stores, the grist- and sawmills, a school, a church and a township hall. One hotel was nicknamed Cupid's, for it was here, local history tells us, that young girls were "scooped up" by local suitors.

Millbridge began its decline when Highway 62 bypassed the village in the early 1960s. Larger towns like Bancroft and Madoc were within easier reach and Millbridge's businesses began to fail. Infertile farmlands chased many farmers from their land.

While Highway 62 has replaced the Hastings Road as the main road north from Belleville to Bancroft, Millbridge Road still traces the original Hastings Road alignment and here the ghost town of Millbridge can be found. Today, most of the ghosts of Millbridge lie beside the old Hastings Road from Millbridge Centre Road to north of West Road. Several original buildings have survived here, many in seasonal use. At the one-time centre of town, the former hotel and "East End" store face each in a classical ghost town pose. Both at one time offered gas. The school at the north end has been converted to a house, as has the church at the south end.

When the Central Ontario Railway added its tracks in 1884, it located its Millbridge station about 8 km (5 miles) to the east. Around the little wooden station grew a railway satellite community named Millbridge Station, with a few homes for rail workers, a store and the grand brick Hogan's Hotel to accommodate train travellers. Dennis Hogan operated a post office here until 1908, which Ella Hogan continued until the 1940s.

Today, the well-maintained building is the community's only surviving structure and has become a private home. The railway right of way is now the Hastings Heritage Snowmobile Trail. The hotel lies on the Stoney Settlement Road east of Highway 62.

While most of the other original stopping places have been replaced by country homes or have vanished completely, Millbridge and Millbridge Station offer ghostly vestiges of days long gone whose passing was lamented as early as 1925.

Log ruins abound at the completely abandoned mountaintop settlement of Newfoundout.

NEWFOUNDOUT

In 1856 the Opeongo Road, the first of Ontario's colonization routes, wound its way up the face of the Black Donald Mountains, a granite ridge that stretches like a mighty wall across the south edge of the Ottawa Valley. Below, the farm lands were generally level and productive. But above the craggy peaks, the lands were strewn with monster boulders, many the size of a house. Despite the obstacles, settlers cleared the land and tilled the stony soil.

At intervals of roughly every ten lots, side roads were surveyed up to the summits to allow settlers to access these remote plateaus. Near an intersection known as Davidson's Corners, a dozen settlers turned off the Opeongo Road and struggled up the mountainside, where they located their lots and began to clear the land. They called their community Newfoundout, although the post office went by the less colourful name of Donohue.

For several years, 13 farm families lived and toiled on Newfoundout's harsh soils. While no town ever grew, services such as sawmilling and blacksmithing were offered on local farms. But the community failed to attract schools or churches, and children had to walk each day down the treacherous mountain trail to the nearest school. Gradually, the remoteness, combined with impossible farming conditions, proved too much for the farmers and by 1948 everyone had left; Newfoundout became a totally ghosted settlement.

It could almost be called a "lost" settlement. The road to it is a steep trail up the side of the mountain, generally impassable for passenger vehicles, and a steep hike on foot. On top of the plateau, the trail levels off and the first of the ghost farms appears, followed by the log cabins and barns that formed the nucleus of the community. Today most of them sit roofless and overgrown, while a rusting car hulk lies in the tall grass beside them. From here the road divides, and leads another 4 km (2.5 miles) to more ruined farm homes and collapsed barns.

The road to Newfoundout begins at the intersection of the Constant Road 3 with the Opeongo Road, 5 km (3 miles) west of Highway 41.

PORT MILFORD

Port Milford was just one of more than a dozen ports that ringed the shores of Prince Edward County. Its location in the sheltered waters of South Bay, a protected harbour on the southeast coast of the island, 16 km (10 miles) south of Picton, gave it a natural advantage for both shipbuilding and exporting.

Port Milford dates from the arrival from Kingston in the 1860s of James and William Cooper, who built docks, stone warehouses and a general store. When Earl Collier arrived, James Cooper built him a fine red brick house, which stands to this day. Collier went on to operate the general store after the turn of the century.

A short distance along the shore, A.W. Minaker opened a store, hotel and wharf. By the 1880s Cooper owned these as well.

An active shipbuilding industry soon developed, where George Dixon built the *W.R. Taylor* in 1877, and the McMurphy brothers the *Huron*. Other schooners launched at Cooper's wharf included the *Jennie Lind, Jessie Brown, Marysburg, C.J. Collier, C. Gearing* and *Speedwell*. To guide these ships into the harbour, there hung only a lantern on a pole. The remains of the *Fleetwood*, one ship that did not make it, still lie in the offshore waters of the bay.

In its heyday as a port, Port Milford shipped butter, cheese, lumber, apples and barley. Although the little port could handle the smaller schooners popular in the mid-1800s, it could not accommodate the larger steamers that began plying the lakes toward the end of the century. After the railway reached Picton, most of the smaller ports along the county's coast faded.

By 1900 Port Milford's shipping days were over. With the growth of vegetable production across the county, the Church brothers selected Port Milford as a site for a large cannery. By the 1930s the Canadian Canning Company operated the plant, and Port Milford became larger and more active than in its heyday as a port. Its population edged up to 100, and along its main streets stood nearly two dozen buildings plus the store, the church and the school.

But in the late 1930s the cannery closed. Only an overgrown foundation remains where the cannery stood, and on the house-lined road that once led to it, only grassy mounds abut a dirt track. At the water's edge, Cooper's stone warehouses are reduced to foundations and the wharves to piles of lumber. On the shore of the harbour, Earl Collier's fine brick house still dominates. Opposite it stands the vacant general store, its name still vaguely visible. The site of the port lies at the end of Collier Rd., a short distance south of County Rd 13 and about 15 km (9 miles) from the thriving town of Picton.

As this view shows, the harbour at Port Milford wasn't always a busy one.

Left: Port Milford's former store has survived decades of abandonment.

A few railside buildings survive on the abandoned right of way for the Kingston & Pembroke Railway, where it accessed Wilbur's thriving iron mines.

WILBUR

When the tracks of the pioneer Kingston & Pembroke Railway line twisted their way into North Frontenac's rugged hills, the railway gave access to resources of timber and minerals, including a substantial iron deposit. With its large reserve of ore, the Wilbur mine became the leading iron producer on the KPR. By 1888 the town had some 250 residents, most of them miners who toiled for the Kingston and Pembroke Iron Mining Company and lived in company cabins or boarding houses near the mine site. More than just a company town, Wilbur included Dave Tait's blacksmith shop and William Caldwell's general store, as well as a shingle mill, a carpentry shop and a shoe emporium.

An edition of the *Renfrew Mercury*, dated May 5, 1887, reported: "The chief pit at the mine of Wilbur is 220' deep. The daily output before was about 100 tons per day. The capacity will be increased to 250 tons by improvements to machinery." The report added that the American syndicate that owned the iron deposits along the KPR boasted land holdings in excess of 15,000 acres (6,000 hectares). The Wilbur mine was their most productive, shipping an estimated 125,000 tons of ore between 1886 and 1900.

The hilly terrain forbade a neatly designed town. The houses and shops lined two sides of a road that twisted across the tracks and on to the mine, 500 metres (550 yards) away. In addition, a small station, rail workers' cabins and a few buildings lay alongside the track itself. By the lake near the mine there were two bunkhouses.

One winter night in 1887 the mine experienced tragedy. The *Renfrew Mercury* of February 25 reported that five men were crushed to death at 1:30 a.m.: "A huge slide of earth weighing many tons was without an instant warning precipitated from the roof upon a number of miners who were working around the skip car. Those who escaped death sounded the alarm, which was quickly responded to, and the work of rescuing those alive and recovering the bodies of those killed began. Five men were directly under the centre of the mass where it fell and were all taken out dead. Long before the bodies were recovered the wives, children and other relatives of the unfortunate dead had assembled at the mine and many heartrending scenes occurred."

The iron deposit soon began to dwindle, and in 1911 the mine closed. The station and post office soon followed. As the miners and businesses moved away, Wilbur became a ghost town.

Two original buildings still stand at the railway right of way. One bears the station name board, although the station itself was moved to a lake farther south. Most of the mine houses were removed as they and the village's places of business degenerated into foundations, cellar holes and scattered lumber hidden by advancing underbrush. The ghost village lies at the end of the Wilbur Road, a forest track that leads south from the railway town of Lavant Station on the Lavant Road about 10 km (6 miles) east of Highway 508.

The saw- and gristmills of Traverston had both ceased operations by the time of this early image.

CHAPTER 2

TRAILS TO THE WEST

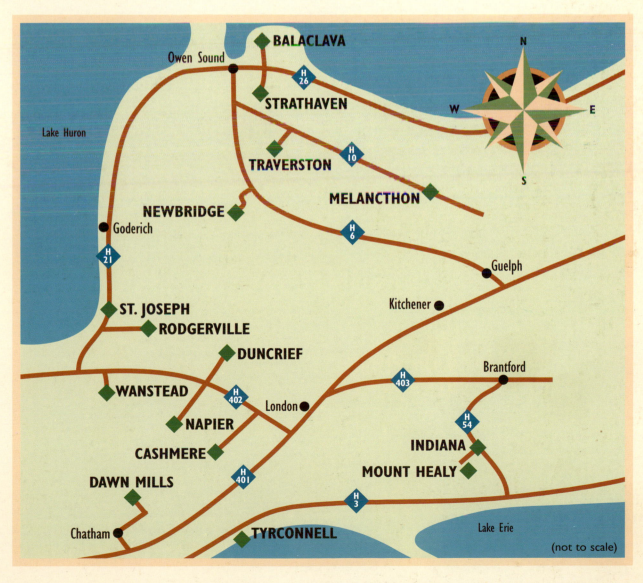

A few vacant buildings are still
managing to survive in Balaclava.

BALACLAVA
(Grey County)

The three Ontario communities that bore the name of Balaclava strangely have all become ghost towns. The former sawmill town of that name lies in the heart of Renfrew County and is described in the previous chapter. Another, located on Highway 9 between Chatsworth and Markdale, has disappeared under highway widening. The third lies in Grey County northeast of Owen Sound.

Grey County's Balaclava began around 1850 when George Scott built a sawmill on Waterton's Creek. Later, Alex Reid and Joseph Frizzel added stores nearby, while Charles Brown and Duncan Cameron operated blacksmith shops, and Elijah Moulton a hotel.

The growing village soon added Alex McMullen's wagon factory and John Lusk's carpenter shop, while Duncan Cameron, Elijah Cross, George Johnson and W. Moulton added blacksmith shops that operated at various times. In 1864 a school opened, with Simon Grantham as its first teacher. Following a fire, classes were held in the nearby Orange Hall until a new stone schoolhouse could be built. It in turn was replaced in 1915 with a brick school building. In 1912 telephone service was added to the area,

a three-party system that lasted independently until 1960, when it joined the Bell Telephone company system. Despite these services and facilities, Balaclava residents never enjoyed their own churches and had to travel to nearby places of worship.

At its peak, the population of Balaclava never amounted to more than seventy-five. Gradually, over the years, the forests gave way to farms. The railway lines bypassed the area in favour of Owen Sound. As the shops and mills shut down, the post office struggled on, until it finally closed in 1961.

The former store and post office were located in the inn, an attractive brick building built in 1875, which still stands on the southeast corner of the intersection, although it has been much altered. Other abandoned structures on the northwest side of the intersection, and a couple of additional early-occupied dwellings round out the community today. Foundations of a few other structures can be seen south of the intersection.

To reach Balaclava, follow the 2nd Concession Road north from Highway 10 about 8 km (5 miles) to Lakeshore Drive, the location of the community.

Only this bend in the road, which follows
Cashmere's street pattern, hints that a busy
mill community once stood here.

CASHMERE

Somewhere in a cornfield on the banks of the brown Thames River near the village of Wardsville are the ghosts of a town where shops and mills once flourished and several houses once stood. Cashmere dates from 1825 when Singleton Gardiner moved from Port Talbot on Lake Erie to the banks of the Thames. Here he purchased a large tract of land, dammed the river, and set up a saw- and gristmill. On nearby Longwoods Road he built an inn.

In 1856 Gardiner's son William hired surveyor Crosbie Brady to lay out a village plan with streets named Queen, William, James and Main. Bridge Street led to the spot where Gardiner proposed to bridge the river, while Mill Street led to the busy mills. By 1860 Cashmere could claim not just Gardiner's mills, which by then included two more sawmills and a blacksmith shop, but also a sash factory and a cabinetmaker, as well as other sawmills and blacksmiths. Henry Fleming and Christopher Hendershott operated taverns, and the population of the town was estimated at 100.

A dam across the river to power the mills infuriated residents upstream, who felt the structure was impairing their fishing. The Ontario government soon came to their rescue and removed it. Later efforts to build a bridge at Cashmere, however, were thwarted when one was built further downstream at Clachan.

In 1880 yet another scheme fell by the wayside when a proposal to link Cashmere with London by steamer service was dashed after the tragic sinking of the steamer *Victoria* near London in 1881.

Because it lay within the flood plain of the Thames River, Cashmere was a frequent victim of spring floods. One of the worst inundations occurred in 1876 when an early break-up of the ice on the river left the village under 5 feet of water. This, along with the arrival of the railways elsewhere, doomed the little village, which a visitor in the 1880s described as being in ruins. By 1911 the mill sites and village lots had been sold off to adjacent farmers, and today the site is covered with corn.

Cashmere Road lies 6 km (3.5 miles) west of the village of Wardsville. It leads south from County Road 2 and after 500 metres (550 yards) it bends sharply to reflect the original town plan. Near the bend, some concrete curbs can yet be seen. The cemetery is on the Longwoods Road, which is County Road 2.

DAWN MILLS

A mid the farm fields east of Chatham, Dawn Mills' few surviving structures remain in use, although it still contains the ghosts of its former greatness.

In 1837, as the land along the Sydenham River was opening for settlement, William Taylor and James Smith built saw- grist- and woollen mills on the banks of the Sydenham River, just a few kilometres upstream from what was then the busy town of Dresden. Until that time farmers had been forced to take their grain by canoe as far as Detroit. The earliest road wound its way along the bank of the Sydenham River, linking mill villages such as Shetland, Croton and the now-vanished community of Smiths Falls (not to be confused with the town of Smiths Falls in eastern Ontario).

Dawn Mills' future looked so promising that a village plan was laid out with six streets and several dozen lots. Along them were a pair of stores, three hotels and a church. With its population of 100, it challenged Dresden for regional supremacy and for a time was the township's judicial centre. Then, in the 1850s, the railways began crossing the fertile countryside and bypassed the little mill town, with the Great Western passing to the south through Chatham, then the Grand Trunk to the north. Other lines made their way through Dresden and Wallaceburg, drawing businesses, travellers and industries from the riverside villages to the noisy new railway towns. Like so many others, Dawn Mills became a backwater and lost its industries.

But the ghosts of Dawn Mills' busier days still lurk. On the west side of today's Dawn Mills Road, a former hotel and an old residence hide in a dead end lane, which was once the main riverside route into Dresden. On the east side of the road is the church, now the Old Calvary Mennonite Church, and the former parsonage. These two buildings face away from the present road onto what was once Dawn Mills' main street, a street now marked only by a row of mature trees. Nearby, a few old cellar holes hark back to residences in now-vacant lots, while south of the church, the cemetery remains open and maintained.

The village lies 5 km (3 miles) east of Dresden on Dawn Mills Road, 2 km (1.2 miles) north of Highway 21. While the river road to Dresden is now closed west of Dawn Mills, a scenic riverside drive leads along the Sydenham River to the northeast.

Dawn Mills' church and one-time manse
face onto a lawn that previously the
village's main street.

Left: Now a residence, the former Dawn
Mills Hotel sits on a lane that was once
the main route to Dresden.

An early house still stands in
Duncrief, its last. Its plaque
announces its date as 1837.

DUNCRIEF

The waters of the little creek have nearly dried up; the one-time yards by the road are choked with weeds and tall grass. Were it not for the bulge on the river bend that was once the old mill dam, and the weathered abandoned house beside the road, time would have erased all signs that Duncrief was once the milling centre for dozens of pioneer farmers.

Duncrief began in 1835 on land owned by Joseph and Robert Charlton where Jeremiah Robson built a sawmill. Five years later Joseph Charlton added a flourmill, which his sons operated until 1886. "The mill was a great centre in the community," wrote Dr. S.E. Charlton in his *History of the Charlton Family.* "Wheat was brought from the country round about and ground into flour, teamed and sold at Ailsa Craig." He noted that the mill dam frequently broke and "there would be a great rallying of neighbours and relatives to restore it."

When the mill burned in 1895, the community again rallied to rebuild it. But the community was not unanimous about the dance held in the mill upon its completion: "Some criticism was indulged in over a dance which was held in the mill ... the wisdom of such an entertainment is a question of opinion ... the young men had all worked hard helping to erect the mill and it would have been small potatoes to have refused them an evening's enjoyment."

Finally, when the dam washed out yet again in 1908, the mill ceased operations for good. Duncrief also attracted a handful of other businesses and residences, including a store and a post office that operated until about 1910, and several different blacksmiths.

The village's lone church, a white frame building, was gone by 1895. The threat of floods has continued to keep new development from the flood plain of the valley, leaving only overgrown yards, the foundations of the mill dam and a solitary abandoned house. Because traffic has found other more convenient routes, the old mill road to the site has remained a seldom-used dirt lane. The old frame house appears to be maintained, although unoccupied, and bears a plaque dated "1837." The mill foundation is also vaguely perceptible in the bushes on the east side of the road.

Duncrief is about 15 km (9 miles) northwest of London. Mill Road to Duncrief lies between Concession Roads 10 and 11 of Lobo Township, about 1 km (0.6 miles) west of New Ontario St.

The only evidence of Duncrief's vital mill site is this riverside remnant.

Indiana's grandest home, Ruthven, was
built by David Thompson, who founded
the lockside community on the Grand
River Canal.

INDIANA

Before the arrival of the railway era in the nineteenth century, Canada relied for transportation upon its water highways and the canals that linked them. While canals along the Rideau, Trent, Niagara, St. Lawrence, and St. Mary's rivers still function, the canal that opened in 1832 on the Grand River has largely been forgotten and most evidence of it lost.

To open the Grand River to navigation and to access the pine stands and the gypsum deposits in the riverbanks, the Grand River Navigation Company during the 1830s constructed a canal between Brantford and Lake Erie. A series of six locks bypassed the few rapids and falls that impeded its flow. Villages sprouted at many of the locks – villages like York, Middleport and Caledonia, all of which thrive today and all of which contain historic buildings that date from the canal era.

Indiana, however, was not so fortunate. Located at Lock #1, it had grown by 1846 from a saw- and gristmill site into a "village of 120 inhabitants [with] a Catholic church … grist mill, two saw mills, distillery, two stores, two taverns" and other businesses, according to a contemporary observer. A town plan contained 117 lots on ten streets. As canal traffic increased, Indiana grew to contain 30 industries and 300 residents at its peak.

The Mussen brothers and James Kirkland both operated distilleries, David Thompson and Lester the grist- and sawmills. From his pail factory, Lester shipped 50 dozen pails to Hamilton each week. A Mr. Young and his family hand-operated a little swing bridge over the narrow canal. A bridge 150 m (500 feet) long spanned the Grand River River itself. Jacob Wigg's daily stages linked Indiana with the riverside towns of Cayuga, York and Caledonia, with fares as low as 10 cents a ride. Although it enjoyed two churches, by far the most frequented was the Catholic church; many of the town's inhabitants were of Irish background with names like Farrel, Kinnear, McKenna, McClory, McMullen and Miles Finlan.

The man responsible for most of the industries was David Thompson. He laid out the town, owned most of the industries and celebrated his prosperity by building a grand pillared mansion that he named Ruthven on the banks of the river at the south end of the town. He operated a farm of nearly 1,500 acres (600 hectares) around the house. The property today forms the Ruthven National Historic Park, which is owned and operated by the Lower Grand River Land Trust Inc.

Indiana's decline began in the 1850s, when the Great Western Railway began to build its line into south-

From a town with 400 residents,
only a single house survives intact.

western Ontario. Canal traffic virtually stopped, and businesses shipped goods by the faster year-round rail. While most of the canal's lock villages became quiet backwaters, Caledonia and Cayuga received rail service and prospered. However, Indiana died.

In 1879 it was noted in the *Illustrated Historical Atlas of the Counties of Haldimand and Norfolk* that, although Indiana "had grown into brief importance while the old navigation company existed, [it] dropped into decay and dilapidation when those temporary causes of prosperity were removed." By 1900 only 25 people were left.

Of the houses and the streets, only two remain. The Gingerbread Inn and Bar is said to incorporate three of the early houses. Just one original house survives with its exterior only slightly altered; the Hill House, as it is known, was built in the 1830s and is now owned by Ruthven Park.

Thompson's mansion, which remained in the family until the 1990s, is now a national historic site and is being carefully restored as funds allow. It is open to the public for tours. The Thompson family cemetery rests behind a cast-iron fence to the south of the mansion. West of the mansion, archaeology students have excavated much of the Indiana town site, including the grave markers of the long-buried "Irish" cemetery.

What were once the village streets have become driveways or, in the case of the main road from the mansion to the town, a hiking trail. Evidence of the mill and the lock still lingers in the overgrowth on the side of the riverbank, while terracing of the cabins and traces of the streets have been demarked throughout.

Ruthven Park, with the ghost town of Indiana, lies on Brant Road 54 (a "scenic parkway") about 5 km (3 miles) north of the village of Cayuga.

An historical sketch shows the mill and lock station at Indiana. *(Historical Atlas for the County of Haldimand and Norfolk.)*

MELANCTHON

Along the Sydenham Road, a settlement road that led pioneers to their distant farm lots in Grey County (an area of wilderness then known as the Queen's Bush), a string of small hotels used to serve travellers' most basic needs. Hastily constructed of logs or lumber, they provided meals and accommodation for travellers weary of the jolting stage coach journeys. At the hamlet of Melancthon they could choose from Beachell's and O'Boles' hotels. In 1870, as the tracks of the Toronto, Grey & Bruce Railway were being laid from Orangeville to Owen Sound, J.W. Morey added another hotel, known as the Bruce, and the growing village gained a store and a blacksmith shop as well.

By 1890, with trains puffing regularly along the TG&B, the village experienced a modest "boom," adding a new store and hotel, a Methodist church, a school and an Orange Hall. Near the small wooden railway station, stood a sawmill, a grain elevator and a few houses. The mill owner, James Sloan, also built a few small cabins to accommodate his workers and their families. So impressed was a local newspaper reporter that he gushed, "A stranger arriving from the station would think himself in the suburbs of a city."

Following the First World War, Melancthon's businesses and functions began to close. Shelburne was larger and began to attract the area's residents. The auto age brought an end to much of the railway's business. One by one, the mills, the elevator, the station and even the rails themselves disappeared. The town hall, the Orange Lodge and the church are nowhere to be seen, while the gravestones in the cemetery have all been rearranged in tight formation.

The former general store and a single early dwelling are Melancthon's sole remaining structures. Some overgrown lots by the abandoned crossing are the only clues that this was the economic heart of a once-bustling village. Government has foolishly allowed the CPR to remove its tracks, destroying yet another opportunity to offer a future transportation alternative to the increasing congestion and pollution created by trucks and cars.

Melancthon is on Highway 10, 6.5 km (3.5 miles) northwest of Shelburne at County Road 17. The store sits on the northeast corner, while the site of the railway station is about 500 metres (550 yards) west on County Road 17.

Much of Melancthon was centred around the station and feed mills located at the now-abandoned railway right of way.

Melancthon's rearranged gravestones suggest that the village was once much more populated than at present.

MOUNT HEALY

With the opening of the Grand River Canal in 1835, several canal-side industries were established, and villages often grew around them. By 1850 Mount Healy had developed around a sawmill and plaster mill and included a blacksmith shop, carriage shop and hotel. Plaster deposits were extensive on the shores of the Grand River, and one of the largest mills was that built by John Donaldson at Mount Healy.

Plaster was being mined here as early as 1846, extracted from the banks of the Grand River near the historic hamlet of York. The plaster was ground for fertilizer, calcinated plaster and water lime plaster. By 1870, with its population peaking at 170, Mount Healy was the largest village in the township. Teams of horses and oxen hauled grain from throughout the township to the gristmills by the river, while logs that had been rolled into the river were winched along a track to the sawmill.

Millworkers boarded in the two-storey brick hotel built in 1865 by Henry Dochstadter. The store and post office in it were operated by Andrew Donaldson, a nephew of John Donaldson, and the enterprise offered two long sheds for the tired teams of horses. Business directories of the day listed four blacksmiths, a cooper, two wagon makers, and a carpenter among the villages other entrepreneurs.

A dam a short distance upstream and two smaller dams at the village itself, operated by the Grand River Navigation company, provided power for the mills, for which Donaldson had to pay 72 pounds 10 shillings per year. As the navigation company that operated the canal began to lose more money, as a result of competition from the railways, the dams fell into disrepair, and steam engines were imported to operate the mills.

The village consisted of a main street that led back from the river, along which were the mills by the wharf, a store, a school and the homes of Donaldson and A.W. Thompson. A side street led to the dozen cabins built for

The Donaldson mill was one of the main industries in Mount Healy.

the mill workers. At the end of that street stood what was then – and still is – one of the most elegant buildings on the banks of the Grand River, Henry Dochstadter's large two-storey brick hotel.

By 1869 Mount Healy had a 150 inhabitants. Gypsum and lumber were loaded onto barges for their journey upriver to Brantford, where the canal ended, or downriver to Port Maitland on Lake Erie.

Eventually the pine was depleted, the plaster mill became uneconomical, and, following the influx of the railways, the canal ceased operation. Mount Healy died, and the stores and cabins gradually disappeared. But the hotel has remained and ranks as one of the most impressive sights along the river.

In the 1960s and 1970s, as modern country homes inundated the banks of the Grand, David Olsen bought the old hotel and renovated it into a home, a use it continues to enjoy. The massive brick building dominates the Grand River's west shoreline about 4 km (2.5 miles) south of the village of York.

The road that passes the former hotel today follows a route different from the one Donaldson would have known. Rather than hug the riverbank and turn in front of the hotel as it did a century ago, today's route bends inland and passes behind it. Beside the hotel in a field through which the old road once passed, bushes and young trees cover the vague cellar holes of the village itself. South of the hotel and village site, a board and batten house represents the last of the village homes. Mud Road (an appropriate name) leads west to the tiny cemetery where many members of the Donaldson and Dochstadter families lie interred.

Mount Healy is on River Road 3.5 km (2 miles) south of Regional Road 9, which crosses the Grand River at the hamlet of York. While not a ghost town, York has remained a relic village that was once the site of a lock and mills. Early churches and a one-time hotel still stand in this picturesque village.

Top: Only this single house sits on what was once Mount Healy's main street, which led to the mills and the wharf.

Mount Healy's main riverside road has been rerouted from the front of a grand house that was once the village's Dochstadter Hotel.

Napier's former store now sits
vacant, the last of the once-busy
mill town's ghostly remnants.

NAPIER

Army settlements in western Ontario were few. However, in 1829 a disbanded military unit was given land along both banks of the Sydenham River and by 1838 had constructed a log school, a church and a military academy. A few years later, the tide of settlers swept into the watershed, and in 1852 Colonel John Arthur and an entrepreneur named Keefer, recognizing the excellent supply of timber and waterpower in Napier, erected the first grist- and sawmills. Shortly afterward, the J.G. Sutherland Company moved in, acquired the mills and built a modern woollen mill. The list of industries grew and by 1870 the little towns could count a pump factory, a brickyard, a wagon factory, three blacksmiths and a tinsmith. Two practising physicians offered their services as well. Napier's town plan spread over 120 lots on 10 streets.

High Market Street, the main thoroughfare, was lined with two hotels (the Napier Inn and the Sydenham House) and three stores, as well as by wagon and blacksmith shops, most clustered around the main intersection at Arthur Street. A handsome brick Wesleyan Methodist church was built on the south bank of the river overlooking the village.

A local advertisement in the *Strathroy Age* of 1870 offers a rare snapshot of the village: "Gentlemen, good wheat, wool and saw logs are in good demand at the Napier mills for cash or goods, etc." But the same newspaper must have sensed that the end could not be far off for it announced: "Several good lots of land are for sale cheap for cash or on terms." Clearly, Sutherland's lots were not selling as briskly as he had hoped.

But Sutherland's mills dominated the town. He was willing to sell or barter "for cash or goods." Among the goods that his mills provided were "flour, cloths, lumber, chopped feed manufactured to order and sold on most reasonable terms."

Along one side of Napier's main street, the visitor would find the cheese factory, the wagon factory and blacksmith, the Masonic Hall and the cabinet shop, all forming the south end business district. Lining the opposite side were the tinsmith, and another wagon factory and blacksmith. The Napier Inn and the Presbyterian church stood close together near the lip of the valley, while partway down the valley wall stood Calvert's store with the Sydenham House hotel nearby.

In the section of town north of the river, the visitor would continue on to find three more stores and the union hall and post office, along with the cabins and homes of the mill workers.

By the 1880s railways were starting to take their toll on crossroads hamlets and little mill towns. Napier, like others, began a downward slide to a ghost town status that even more recent redevelopment hasn't entirely obliterated.

A newer road alignment cuts across the old street plan. However, the old school, the church and a few original dwellings still stand, marking the locations of the original streets. Although a number of newer homes now occupy Sutherland's old town lots, the vacant general store lends a spectral air to this increasingly active "ghost" town.

Napier lies on the Napier Road 1 km (0.6 miles) north of Winter Road and 15 km (10 miles) southwest of Strathroy via County Roads 9 and 2.

Relaxation time at the Newbridge
general store in the 1890s.

NEWBRIDGE

As settlers made their way through the forests of western Ontario to their newly acquired farm lots, mills were quickly built by the waterpower sites on the area's many rivers. One source of waterpower was the Maitland River, which begins near Harriston and tumbles toward Lake Huron. For most of its length, the flow of the river is fast and steady, offering ideal conditions for the growth of many little mill villages along its banks.

In 1854 William Spence, along with two other settlers, John Wiggins and James Kerr, arrived at the banks of the river in Howick Township and bought a 500-acre parcel of land. Here they laid out a townsite that they called Spencetown, with lots located along its only two streets, Mill and Main.

In 1860 Charles Ferrand arrived from Quebec and built the area's first gristmill, adding a flourmill a short time later. It too ended up in the Spence family. James Carson built the town's first store where William McLauglin opened the post office. However, because another post office in eastern Ontario already had a similar name, McLauglin changed the name to Newbridge, after a village in Ireland. A man named Johnson opened the first tavern in 1864.

Newbridge was soon a bustling country town rivalling such nearby communities as Fordwich and Gorrie. It added a church, a school, an Orange Lodge and a couple of blacksmiths. The population gradually increased from 130 in 1872 to 200 a decade later. But when the Teeswater branch of the Toronto, Grey & Bruce Railway passed further north through Fordwich, Newbridge became a backwater even though a daily stage service linked the two towns. By 1900 the population had declined by half, and only nine buildings remained on the main street

In 1922 fire destroyed the mills and later Johnson's hotel and the store. The Orange Lodge and the church ceased operation, while the other small shops were burned or demolished.

The church and the manse still stand, both used as private residences, and some modern homes have been added in recent years. Meanwhile, the old mill road is now an overgrown line of shrubs, the site of the mills barely discernible. Close by, the Orange Lodge stands vacant.

Newbridge is situated on Maple Lake Line about 5 km (3 miles) south of Bruce County Road 57 and 12 km (7.5 miles) southwest of the village of Harriston.

Newbridge's quiet main street is a far cry from its busier days as a mill village.

RODGERVILLE

In 1848, when Matthew Rodger made his way up a crude trail known as the London Road, settlers were just beginning to clear the forests that covered their farm lots. In that year, Rodger built a double house, part of which served as a hotel named the Western Hotel, and part as a general store. Next to the store he added a blacksmith shop and carriage works, and seven years later he started a brickmaking operation that employed 22 men.

By 1863 Rodgerville's main street contained two hotels, two stores, three blacksmiths, two shoemakers, a butcher, a cooper and a wagon maker. A Presbyterian church with a congregation numbering 100 stood a short distance north. Known as the Rodgerville Band of Hope, its congregation carried the temperance message into the area. The Grey Brothers opened a blacksmith and wagon shop, turning out a popular and widely used brand of plough. And in 1870 Andrew Malcolm launched a cheese factory, exporting cheese as far as Scotland and Germany.

These were Rodgerville's palmy days, and few believed her destiny was anything but promising. But early in the 1870s, railway surveyors appeared. The London, Huron & Bruce Railway, it seemed, would run through Rodgerville. At first, expectations rose. However, the Petty brothers, who owned land and mills 2.5 km (1.5 miles) to the north, offered their land, and the station was built at Hensall instead.

This decision initiated the decline of the roadside village. As it was more profitable for industry to locate by a station, Hensall grew into a thriving railway town. One by one the businesses in Rodgerville closed and the buildings became vacant. Matthew Rodger's old hotel stood empty for several years. In 1886 even the congregation of the Rodgerville Church chose a new site in Hensall. By 1890, its population a mere 45, Rodgerville was down to Bonthron's store and Mcleod's blacksmith shop. Bonthron's son Robert also opened a store in Hensall. Finally, when the post office closed in 1899, Rodgerville's name all but disappeared from maps.

Today, only three original buildings still stand. The three survivors, spaced well apart, along with a few modern homes, now give the ghost community the look of just another country road experiencing modern countryside development. One of the houses has been extensively renovated and another re-sided, while the third stands vacant and surrounded by shrubs.

The London Road has evolved into busy Highway 4, and Rodgerville lies a short distance south of Rodgerville Road, the first intersection south of Hensall. The cemetery lies about 250 metres (200 yards) east along this side road. A sign at the entrance to a private lane stating "Rodgerville" is the only other visible evidence that the place ever existed.

Only three houses, similar in style to this, survive
on a busy highway that was once the main street
of a bustling pre-railway village.

ST. JOSEPH

Anyone searching for Narcisse Cantin's dream city of St. Joseph today will inevitably end up at a small park beside the site of this ghost town's largest building, the Balmoral Hotel. Otherwise, there is little to show that St. Joseph was once destined to be a major Lake Huron town. Yet the hotel was the only part of the grand scheme by would-be railway and canal builder Narcisse Cantin that was realized … and even it failed.

During the 1840s the fertile clay plains of southern Huron County, stretching to the shores of Lake Huron, had become the destination of Quebec's crowded and poor farmers. Among them was Antoine Cantin. On a small creek, Moses Johnson built the area's first sawmill and the community became known as Johnson's Mills. It attracted a church, a general store, a post office and the Queens Hotel. In 1857 optimistic landowners laid out an impressive townsite and named their future metropolis Lakeview. But the site remained undeveloped.

Antoine's son Narcisse, born there in 1870, quickly established himself as an entrepreneur. By the age of 17 he was shipping cattle from the railway town of Zurich, later moving his operation to Buffalo. Impressed by what he saw of the Erie Canal, he began drawing up plans for a series of canals that would cross Ontario's southwest peninsula and terminate at his hometown of Lakeview. Here he would create a city, populating it with expatriate French Canadians who had meanwhile settled in Chicago.

By 1897 he had taken the old Lakeview plan and enlarged it to 400 lots and 20 streets with such exotic names as Napoleon and Josephine. Park Avenue swept about 2 km (1.2 miles) from the main street to the lake, where it ended at a huge recreational park. He called his city St. Joseph.

St. Joseph grew quickly. In less than a decade Cantin had attracted an organ factory, a winery and a brick works. Beside the old Lakeview store and hotel, he added the Bissonette Block, an office for the professional men of the town. By 1904 the city contained 25 grand homes, many of them three storeys high and built of yellow brick.

Cantin's grand achievement was to be the Balmoral Hotel. He began construction in 1897 and poured a quarter of a million dollars into it. The three-storey yellow brick hotel occupied an entire city block and boasted a 24 metre

Of St Joseph's many buildings, only five survive, including what was once the organ factory.

(80-foot) bar. Advertisements went out from a special office in New York, touting it as a grand recreational hotel.

But the hotel never opened. With resorts in the rocky wilds of Muskoka already open and luring tourists, Huron County's featureless countryside could not compete, and the hotel remained empty.

Narcisse Cantin's other dreams were also dashed. In 1906 he opened a wharf to ship lumber and fish, but waves and ice soon washed it away. He then began to promote a new railway, the St. Joseph & Stratford Radial Railway. Unfortunately, he couldn't regain investor confidence after the failure of his Balmoral Hotel.

In 1914, after 12 years of effort, he managed to incorporate the Great Lakes and Atlantic Canal and Power Company. Taking a leap into the future, he recognized the potential of electrical power and switched his emphasis from the canal to electricity, but the First World War delayed financing. During the 1920s a political scandal involving the government of the day, and power development initiatives on the St. Lawrence River killed yet another Cantin dream.

St. Joseph stagnated. One by one its businesses closed, and in 1920 the Balmoral Hotel was torn down, its elegant furnishings sold to the highest bidder and the bricks used in far less grand buildings. Cantin, diminished from years of grandiose scheming followed by failure, returned to his city and watched it decline until he died in 1940.

It is still possible to find traces of Cantin's dream city. Among the prosperous towns and green fields of Huron County, at the intersection of Highways 84 and 21, about 40 km (25 miles) south of Goderich lies the overgrown site of the Balmoral Hotel. Part of the organ factory is now a craft shop located behind the former Cantin home on Highway 21, where three of St. Joseph's original houses still stand. Between the highway and the lake, a new housing development occupies some of the original streets, many of which bear the names of early francophone settlers. Beside the parkette, Park Avenue also leads to a new housing area and to a private home that was another of St. Joseph's early dwellings.

In the parkette six plaques with early photos describe the fate of the Balmoral Hotel and the wharf, and recount the story of Narcisse Cantin and his failed dream.

The main street in St. Joseph was once lined with homes and stores, as shown here in an image from the 1890s. *(County of Huron)*

What was once Strathaven's main
street is now a driveway to a house
that served as the village store.

STRATHAVEN

Over tens of thousands of years the Beaver and Bighead rivers steadily carved their now-spectacular valleys into the limestone layers of the Niagara Escarpment. Their rushing waters ensured many power sites for the early mills of pioneer Ontario, including the saw- and gristmills that became the basis for a busy village in Grey County.

Strathaven's buildings developed along McNab Avenue, a sidestreet linking the 8th Concession Road with the mills, a short distance away. Leading off McNab Avenue were two short cul-de-sacs and a river road where a few shops and residences also sprang up.

Through Strathaven's formative years, J. Thomas and Son operated flour-, saw- and shingle mills, which attracted other shops and trades. After a few years, McNab Avenue boasted two general stores (those of Joseph Long and W.J. McKessock), a blacksmith, a wagon maker, a school, a Baptist church and the Foresters Hall. McKessock's store, according to a 1904 advertisement, offered a wide variety of goods, including "fur coats, caps, gauntlets, imitation fur caps, kid gloves, horse blankets, whips (and) mocassins," and claimed to be "headquarters for fancy China and Christmas toys. Don't fail to see them." For bartering and purchasing, McKessock's issued its own wooden "coins."

A new church, finished in 1900, replaced an earlier frame building which, for the nominal sum of $40, was given to the Foresters as a meeting hall on the condition that no dance ever take place under the roof. Although Strathaven had a strict intolerance of dancing, it placed no restrictions on horse racing, football or baseball. The large track and field on the north side of McNab Avenue was a popular gathering spot for the township's racing and sports aficionados.

With the close of the nineteenth century, urbanization was well underway in Ontario. Owen Sound, just 30 km (18.5 miles) to the northwest, and Meaford, a like distance to the northeast, became the area's retail and industrial centres. Along with many other country villages, Strathaven began its decline. The mills closed, as did the blacksmith and wagon maker. About 1917, Long demolished his store and moved his house to Owen Sound.

By the time of the Great Depression, Strathaven had shrunk to just 10 buildings, including the church, school and Foresters Hall. After the war, more of Strathaven came tumbling down and today it exists virtually in name alone. The school is now a private residence, the mill sites are long disused, and only a house and McKessock's former store remain. The two cul-de-sacs have long been reclaimed by fields of grain, as have the race track and the row of homes that paralleled the river. Only foundations tell of the Foresters Hall, and a rusting baseball cage denotes the sports field. In spite of the surrounding scene of abandonment, the Baptist church remains to this day an active and vital focus for the residents of this scenic North Grey farming area. The village lies about 30 km (18.5 miles) southeast of Owen Sound, on the 4th Concession a short distance north of Massie Road.

The Maitland River now flows unimpeded
past the site of Bodmin's early mills.

SUNSHINE

Sunshine began with a shingle mill erected by Alfred Brown and powered by the swift-flowing Maitland River. He named the little community "Providence." In 1877 Isaac Rogerson converted the mill to steam power and added a chair factory. When George Kirby divided his land into village lots two years later, Sunshine began to attract more residents and businesses.

Among them were blacksmith Richard Webb and Robert Crittenden, who opened a general store that contained a post office. A meeting hall was established for the local Orange Order and the Foresters. A row of small homes sprang up in the village lots, all connected by a boardwalk. At the intersection, a Methodist church was built with a small cemetery beside it.

But when the railways passed Sunshine by, the location failed to draw other industries, and soon only the sawmill remained. When the supply of timber, which had once seemed endless, became exhausted, it too shut down, and in 1900 the mill and mill site were sold off by auction. The post office relocated to a nearby farm and the remaining buildings were removed. Today only the cemetery survives.

At the intersection of Morris Road and Martin Line 8.4 km (5.2 miles) west of Brussels, the pasture where the buildings once stood now displays only vague mounds. On the northwest corner of the intersection, the cemetery gravestones stones tell of the tragic deaths of young children, some only days old, a testimony to the hardships faced by residents of this long-gone mill village.

A Maitland River neighbour of Sunshine, the mill village of Bodmin, has vanished as completely. It began in 1854 when William Harris built a grist- and sawmill on the river, the area's first such industries. Businesses that followed included Walter Smith's general store, a shoe shop and a cabinet factory. Isaac Downey's lime works, which provided the mortar for the settlers' log cabins, lasted from 1889 until 1910. A small string of homes lined the riverbank. Today, most of Bodmin has been ploughed under, with only overgrowth and depressions in the ground offering any suggestion of its former human habitation.

Bodmin stood just south of Brandon Road near the Maitland River Bridge, a short distance west of Marsh Line.

Only the cemetery survives from the early days when Sunshine was a Maitland River mill town.

TRAVERSTON

When the remote forests of the Queen's Bush were finally opened to settlement around 1850, mills soon began to appear to supply the settlers' needs for lumber and flour. With its frequent waterpower sites, the Rocky Saugeen River attracted more than its share of mill villages. Among them was the village of Traverston.

In 1856 Schofield and Collier erected a saw- and gristmill at one such waterpower site on the river. On the plateau south of the river they laid out a townsite with lots for the houses they expected would be built, complete with an industrial sector that would include, in addition to their mills, a cabinet and chair factory and a machine shop. They called their future village Waverley.

Also in 1856, Schofield and Collier sold their holdings to John Travers, who established a post office. But because Ontario already had a post office named Waverley, he bestowed upon the town his own name, which remains on the maps to this day.

Then, the Toronto, Grey & Bruce Railway arrived and built its station in Markdale 9 km (5.5 miles) to the northeast, bypassing Traverston. While new industries chose to locate at railside, the forests were depleted, and wheat farming moved west. Traverston's mills closed and the village became a ghost town.

After the sawmill was demolished, the gristmill remained derelict until the 1970s, when it was purchased and remodelled into a residence. Vestiges of the wooden mill dam remain visible on the river's rapids below the current bridge. In the vicinity of the little ghost town, the forested riverbanks have attracted newer country homes. However, on the old village plot there still stands an occupied original house, a dilapidated cabin and the rubble from a third, which had stood until recent years.

These relics lie on the south bank of the Rocky Saugeen River on Traverston Road south of County Road 12 about 9 km (5.5 miles) west of Markdale.

The saw- and gristmills have both ceased operations by the time of this early image. The sawmill has gone, but the gristmill (right) is now a home.

Traverston's photogenic mill on the Rocky
Saugeen River has been converted to a home.

Tyrconnell's historic Backus-Page house is now a museum.

What was once the site of Tyrconnell's busy fishing industry is now a quiet stretch of beach.

TYRCONNELL

As pioneers began to arrive along Erie's shore, their first and most pressing need was mills … sawmills to provide lumber for houses and barns, and gristmills to turn their grain into flour.

Tyrconnell began to develop in the original "Talbot Settlement" begun by Thomas Talbot when a sawmill was built near the mouth of what was then called Number 9 Creek. The name Tyrconnell was selected by Talbot himself, who named it for his father, the Earl of Tyrconnell, in Ireland.

The first settlers to arrive were three families from Pennsylvania, the Pattersons, the Pearces and the Storeys. Steven Backus arrived the following year. His son Andrew would build Tyrconnell's most distinguished house. Known today as the Backus-Page House, the brick mansion, the township's first brick structure, consists of 72,000 bricks and was completed in 1850.

A short distance to the east St. Peter's Anglican Church was raised in 1827. That same year, a post office was opened, which remained in operation until 1913.

Further west, on the flat lands above the shore cliff, a townsite was laid out beside what had by then become Tyrconnell Creek. The plot consisted of 20 streets and more than 300 lots. A wharf was built near the mouth of the creek to ship out grain. By 1857 Tyrconnell was home to 500 inhabitants. Among its businesses were hotels, stores, sawmills, a soap factory, wool factory, cheese factory, carriage maker, shingle factories, and the usual array of trades such as blacksmith, cobbler, saddler, butcher and tanner. Rev J. Kennedy was the pastor at the historic St. Peter's Church at this time.

Twenty years later, however, the railways bypassed Tyrconnell in favour of Dutton 8 km (5 miles) to the north. Port Stanley to the east received the railways as well, and Tyrconnell lost its importance as a port. The mouth of the creek proved inadequate to handle larger fishing boats, and the village began to shrink. In 1976 its population was listed as just 40.

While ruins are few, Tyrconnell remains a ghost of its early days. St. Peters Church and the Backus-Page House both still stand and are well maintained. The house is administered as a museum by the Tyrconnell Heritage Society, while the church still hosts regular worship. These two structures, along with the pioneer cemetery, are situated east of Currie Road on Lake Road. West of Currie Road lie the remains of the village where the only streets from the original survey are Erie St., George St., Neilson St. and Hill St. Fewer than half a dozen early buildings, with a smattering of newer homes, line these old streets.

Erie Street still leads south to the lake, but now ends in a dirt lane and grassy parking area by the ruins of the old wharf. Where warehouses and other port buildings once stood, overgrown fields have taken over.

Tyrconnell can be found by following County Road 8 south from exit 149 on Highway 401.

WANSTEAD

While the greatest concentration of railway ghost towns lies on Canada's prairies, a few in Ontario call such scenes to mind. One of Ontario's most "prairie-like" ghost towns is Wanstead.

It was laid out in typical prairie fashion by the Great Western Railway in 1858. A grid network of streets appeared beside the tracks with the main street leading to the back door of the station.

Along that street lay the stores, the shops, and a hotel, while the back streets contained the residences. By the track were the Great Western station, a sawmill and, in later years, a feed mill. In 1887 a fire destroyed much of the town, but the buildings were quickly replaced. A much worse fate, however, waited until a few years later.

In December of 1902, a blizzard swept across the flat fields that surrounded the town, reducing visibility to zero. Through the storm raced a passenger train known as the *Chicago Flyer*, crowded with Christmas travellers. So blinding was the swirling snow that the train's engineer failed to see that the order board on the Watford station, west of Wanstead, was warning him that a freight train a short distance ahead was manoeuvring to get onto the

Wanstead siding to allow the speeding *Flyer* to pass and needed just a few more seconds.

The crash roused the villagers into action and they raced to the wreck to help however they could. Thirty-eight people lay dead in the twisted tangle of wood and metal, making it one of Canada's worst train disasters.

Wanstead lay between two other growing communities, Watford and Wyoming. Businesses migrated out, and the church and school closed. The four village streets now contain only half a dozen buildings, including the former store and service station. The earlier railway station was later replaced by a Grand Trunk station, and it survives as the office for the current co-op feed mill. The main street, Layton St., which still leads away from the station, is lined with vacant lots.

Strangely, the tracks are still busy with new buildings housing the co-op operations. Around the ghost village, the farmlands stretch out flat and prairie-like, as the tracks disappear to the horizon. As this is the CNR's main route from Toronto to Michigan, freight trains are frequent, while VIA Rail's Sarnia trains pass by each day as well.

The near-deserted main street of
Wanstead, which once was lined with
stores and homes, led prairie-style to
the railway station.

An early image of South Portage
depicts start-up operations of the
Portage Flyer railway.

CHAPTER 3

COTTAGE COUNTRY
TRAILS

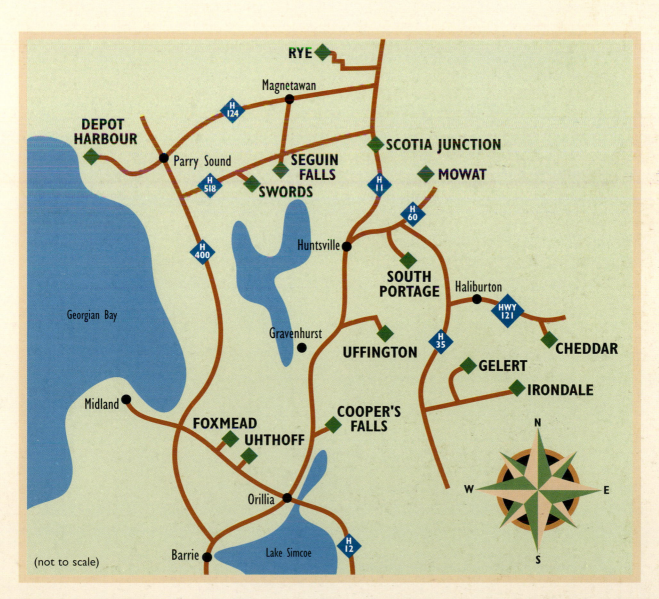

RYE

Magnetawan

H 124

DEPOT
HARBOUR

Parry Sound

SEGUIN
FALLS

SCOTIA JUNCTION

H 518

MOWAT

SWORDS

H 11

H 60

Huntsville

H 400

SOUTH
PORTAGE

Haliburton

Georgian Bay

HWY 121

Gravenhurst

UFFINGTON

H 35

CHEDDAR

GELERT

IRONDALE

Midland

N

FOXMEAD

COOPER'S
FALLS

UHTHOFF

W

E

Orillia

Barrie

Lake Simcoe

H 12

S

(not to scale)

Setting out from Ashdown along the Nipissing Road may
have resembled this early painting, which illustrates travel
in pioneer Ontario. *(Library and Archives Canada)*

ASHDOWN

One of Ontario's most interesting and best-preserved colonization roads is the Nipissing Road. Among the last to be opened, it linked Lake Rosseau at its south end, with Lake Nipissing to the north. Hotels were built at frequent intervals, usually 6 km (3.5 miles) apart, to give weary stage travellers and horses a chance to rest. But the route of the Nipissing Road was difficult and the land poor. Few villages of any size developed. Only Magnetawan, situated on the Magnetawan River and the terminus of a canal from Burks Falls, and Seguin Falls, where J.R. Booth located his busy railway line, grew beyond providing just the basic needs for the surrounding community – a church, a school, a store and a hotel.

The Nipissing Road's most southerly village, Ashdown, developed at its junction with the Parry Sound Colonization Road, 2 km (1.2 miles) west of the village of Rosseau on Lake Rosseau.

Named after pioneer landowners, the village by 1880 boasted a school, an Orange Hall, a Methodist church, a store, and a hotel run by the Ashdown family, as well as R.G. Hall's blacksmith shop and A.H. McCann's wagon and carriage factory. A short distance south of the junction, the White Oak Creek provided power for Thomas Scott's planing mill and Cyrus Lawson's sash and door factory.

Stages departed daily for Parry Sound to the west for $1.25, and twice weekly along the winding Nipissing Road to Magnetawan for $2, and to Nipissing Village for $4.

Ashdown prospered only briefly. With its superior harbour, Rosseau became the new jumping off point for Nipissing Road travellers. Then, the advent of two railways, the Northern Pacific Junction Railway (later the Grand Trunk) line to the east in 1886 and the J.R. Booth's Ottawa, Arnprior & Parry Sound Railway line to the north in 1897, drew both freight and passenger traffic away from the tortuous narrow road. With the decline in road use, Ashdown lost its strategic advantage and its businesses moved to the larger village of Rosseau. By 1908 not even the post office remained.

Visible remains of Ashdown are few and scattered. A log shell, now collapsing, lies behind the site of the former hotel. Depressions and overgrown yards indicate old cellar holes and village lots. Ashdown's pioneer cemetery lies along the Nipissing Road a few metres north of Highway 141.

Little more than a log shell remains at the site of Ashdown, an early Nipissing Road village.

CHEDDAR

During the 1850s the government of Canada West opened the wilds of northern Peterborough and southern Haliburton counties to settlers. From the village of Burleigh the Burleigh Colonization Road wound through the forests for 60 km (37 miles) to meet the Monck Road, an east-west colonization road. By 1870 both the Monck and Burleigh roads had been made more "passable," although it still took a stagecoach half a day to travel 10 km (6 miles). Wayside inns welcomed travel-weary guests with warmth, rest, food and a soft seat after the stagecoach's hard wooden benches. It was at this important road junction in 1871 that Benjamin Woods opened a general store and post office and offered "entertainment to the travelling public."

Woods Corners, as it was known, became the focus for scattered farmers. Besides Woods' store and hotel, James McIlven opened a blacksmith shop, while Lamb and Bates operated sawmills nearby. The hamlet soon added Methodist and Anglican churches and also a school. Around 1890, A. Southwood opened a rival general store and managed to land the post office contract. When the post office opened, Southwood promptly changed the name of the village from Woods Corners to Cheddar after a town in England.

While Cheddar, England, was famous for its cheese, Cheddar, Ontario, became mildly famous for its uranium. About one kilometre (half a mile) south of Woods' old hamlet, uranium lurked in the rocks. For ten years, from 1932 to 1942, the Canada Radium Corporation hammered and banged into the hard rocks. It built a few residences, a company store and a 100-ton mill. Then in 1942, after the deposit had become uneconomical, the company closed shop and left.

Today, Cheddar lies totally abandoned. A sign on Highway 121, 37 km (23 miles) east of Haliburton Village still announces the "Cheddar Road" but it is barely passable save for snowmobiles. The woods have reclaimed both the mine and Woods Corners, and the buildings lie buried in a young forest. Only the one-time boarding house remains solid and is used as a seasonal dwelling. Although its name still appears on maps, Cheddar is a village of the past.

Of Cheddar's early mine
buildings, only the former
boarding house is still around.

The picturesque former Cooper's Falls
blacksmith shop remains a landscape
feature in this once-busy mill town.

COOPER'S FALLS

Although Muskoka's boom in country living continues to creep along the Cooper's Falls Road, the village of that name still retains enough of its ghostly heritage to make for a rewarding visit.

The village owes its origins, as well as its name, to Thomas Cooper who in 1864 showed up with his wife, Emma, and built the area's first, vitally needed, sawmill. In 1878 he opened a store and a post office, which took his name. The village grew around the mill and could soon count a blacksmith, cheese factory, school, and, a short distance from the centre of the village, two churches, one Anglican, the other Methodist.

Along the village streets a number of homes and workers' cabins were built. But the railways passed Cooper's Falls by, focusing instead on Washago about 14 km (8.5 miles) to the west. Here, rail lines such as the Canadian Northern and the Grand Trunk converged, making Washago a major railway junction. Later, as the auto age and the cottage boom swept into Muskoka, the old Muskoka Colonization Road was paved and straightened to become Highway 11, but it too missed Cooper's Falls, likewise going through Washago. Even had transportation trends been friendlier, there are few lakes near Cooper's Falls to have brought much summer tourism to the dwindling little place.

Eventually the mill closed, followed by the school, the post office and the Methodist church. The store and the blacksmith shop stared blankly at each other from across the street. Many of the homes and cabins fell vacant.

Today the village retains a ghost-town aura, with the store and blacksmith shop in place but no longer used. Although many of the original cabins have now been demolished or replaced, a few collapsing shells and weedy lots testify to its former size and activity. While St. George's Anglican Church remains in use, the Methodist church immediately beside it is now silent.

The two churches stand on Cooper's Falls Road at its intersection with the McArthur Sideroad, 8 km (5 miles) east of Washago; the village itself lies a few kilometres further on. Meanwhile, beyond the village, Cooper's Falls Road, which becomes County Road 6, encounters the Black River Road, an old and still winding pioneer trail that ends in the wilderness at the site of the Victoria Colonization Road.

The general store, although no longer functioning, still stands at Cooper's Falls.

Depot Harbour's massive grain elevators were the town's economic lifeline. They burned in 1945.

The most prominent feature in Ontario's largest ghost town is the Roman-like ruin of the former railway roundhouse.

DEPOT HARBOUR

Depot Harbour was the largest Ontario town ever to become a ghost town. At its peak more than 1,600 residents lived in the boarding houses, hotels and 110 dwellings, all carefully laid out on a dozen blocks.

Largely unknown today, John Rudolphus Booth was Ontario's most prominent nineteenth-century lumber baron, owner of the world's largest individually held railway, and at the time Canada's wealthiest man. Born of an Irish farmer on the Yamaska River in Quebec, he moved to the booming lumber town of Ottawa (still known then as Bytown) where he leased a sawmill. After successfully earning the contract to supply lumber for Canada's parliament buildings, he went on to upstage more established lumbermen by winning the rights to the lucrative timber limits in Algonquin Park. In the 1890s he assembled a network of rail lines to link his Ottawa mills to ice-free Atlantic ports, later extending it westward to access his timber stands in faraway Algonquin Park.

Booth then acquired the charter of the Parry Sound Colonization Railway, which completed his link to Georgian Bay, so that he could capture the growing western grain trade. But land prices in Parry Sound, the charter's original terminus, were higher than Booth was prepared to pay, and he changed the route to bypass the town completely. On nearby Parry Island he acquired a parcel of land from the Ojibway band to build his own town. Parry Sound's outraged residents accused Booth of violating the terms of the charter. When Booth discovered that he needed more land, he used the provisions of the *Railway Act* to expropriate it from the band rather than pay fair market price, thereby angering the band members as well.

But Depot Harbour was also one of the deepest and most protected harbours on the great lakes, and here he erected grain elevators, a hotel, boarding houses, a railway roadhouse and 110 family dwellings (some detached, some duplex).

Booth completed his empire with his own fleet of steamers and grain elevators at the American grain ports on the western Great Lakes, a network that provided the shortest grain route from the American west to Atlantic ports.

A string of mill villages grew up along the rail line, many of which became ghost towns following the demise of rail operations. Seguin Falls and Swords, a short distance east of Parry Sound, are two examples, while Mowat in the more distant Algonquin Park thrived briefly on tourism, before it too was abandoned. Booth's divisional point at Madawaska, east of Algonquin Park, sported a roundhouse larger than even that in Depot Harbour, until it was removed in the 1990s for safety reasons. The only other relics of Booth's historic railway empire are the recycled stations at Barry's Bay and Eganville, and a rare wooden water tower, also preserved at Barry's Bay.

As Depot Harbour grew, it added stores, a school, and three churches. Its hockey team competed with teams throughout the Parry Sound area. A company town, Depot Harbour was dry, and thirsty workers had to travel to the hotels and taverns on the outskirts of Parry Sound (also a dry town) located in a noisy little district nicknamed "Parry Hoot."

As the town expanded, it became one of Canada's destinations for European immigrants and numbered among its population 11 different ethnic groups. By 1911 the Census of Canada counted 600 residents in Depot Harbour, a figure that jumped to 1,500 when seasonal workers were in town. To keep entertained, the townsfolk held Saturday dances in the general store, played pool, or skated on the town rink during the long winters.

In 1904 the Grand Trunk Railway bought Booth's holdings for $14.2 million, only to be later taken over by the Canadian National Railway, a special crown agency established to assume Canada's bankrupt railways. With its

Depot Harbour's population
contained enough children to
require a two-storey school
building.

many duplicate lines and facilities, those at Depot Harbour among them, the CNR closed the Depot Harbour roundhouse and amalgamated the shops with those at nearby South Parry.

In 1933 a freak ice floe destroyed a bridge in Algonquin Park. But because the government had already committed its Depression-era funds to the building of Highway 60, the railway was forced to shut down the central portion of Booth's old line. In one blow, Depot Harbour was no longer the shortest route to the Atlantic. Grain shippers began using other ports like Midland and Port McNicoll, and the elevators in Depot Harbour fell into disuse. Then in 1945, a highly volatile supply of cordite being stored nearby caught fire and engulfed the elevators in a midnight fireball that lit the streets of Parry Sound 8 km (5 miles) away.

By 1950, CN had closed the coal dock and planked in the railway bridge, making it easy to drive between the dwindling port and Parry Sound. With the water tanks, the sewers and the streets all desperately needing repair, the CNR simply closed the townsite and sold the houses for $25 each. Many were rebuilt as cottages nearby. The port served briefly as an automated transshipment facility for U.S.-bound iron ore pellets railed in from the Moose Mountain mine north of Sudbury.

Nature has now had 50 years to reclaim the streets and foundations of the old town. In the forest the grey concrete arches of the railway roundhouse, the most visible of the town's vestiges, hover like a Roman ruin.

North of the roundhouse the railway line has become a road to the harbour. Beyond this road the cinder lanes of the old townsite wind westward past the foundation of the railway water tower and those of the houses themselves. It ends at steps that lead to the foundation of the Roman Catholic church, which stands high on a windswept rocky knoll overlooking the waters of the bay. East of the roundhouse, the foundations and old village streets are more hidden by the woods, although a few of the sidewalks are still visible.

The wharf area is busy once more as a boat launch site; the cribbing from the coal dock can still be seen in the waters of the harbour.

When the railway's 99-year lease finally expired, the local First Nations band took over ownership of the townsite. They now use portions of it for ceremonial purposes. The site is about 12 km (7.5 miles) from downtown Parry Sound via the Great North Road to Rose Point. Here Booth's railway swing bridge still links Parry Island with the mainland. From the intersection at the First Nations village, the road then leads west for 3 km (1.8 miles) to an overhead hydro line where the lane to the ghost town forks right.

A collapsed shell marks the location
of the blacksmith shop and other
Foxmead Station buildings.

FOXMEAD STATION

As railway lines threaded their way through Ontario's forests, they attracted mills and their workers' villages to trackside. The stony soils northwest of Lake Simcoe held little hope for farming, but they did contain forests thick with pine trees. It was just such a bounty that lured James Hadden to the route of the Grand Trunk Railway between Orillia and Midland.

In 1878 Hadden erected a large sawmill and added a company village for his workers. The village consisted of two roads. One, along the east side of the tracks, included the mill, a boarding house, a stable, half a dozen cabins for the workers, and a flag station the size of a boxcar.

A second road, on the west side of the tracks, included a blacksmith shop, a store, the mill office and Hadden's home. A union church was soon added a short distance to the west, with a community hall beside it. A school was built a bit further west, although the teachers frequently boarded in Hadden's own house. When it opened, the post office took its name from the area's first two settlers, John Fox and John Mead.

While it lasted, the post office too was located in the Hadden house. But Hadden, it was said, was not an easy man to get along with, and a petition soon began circulating to move the post office to Bradley's Corners about 3 km (1.8 miles) to the west. Following a hearing on the move, tempers abated and the post office stayed put for another 40 years.

At its peak in the 1890s, Foxmead included a store, a mill, a church, a lime kiln, a blacksmith shop and a population of 100 souls.

Shortly afterward, the village began to decline. In 1901 Hadden sold the store, and in 1903 the mill. The store and post office were moved to the Fitzgerald house on the north side of the Foxmead Road, where it would operate for several more years.

But by the 1940s, Foxmead's days were over. The post office and store were then moved to Bradley's Corners and the village buildings were removed. One of the last to go was the station, which was loaded onto a flatcar in 1970 and moved to an undisclosed location.

Today, Bradley's Corners has even taken over the name Foxmead. The railway tracks are now a cinder trail, while the village roads are but vague paths. To the east of the railway right of way, only vague depressions in the field suggest that the village ever stood here. To the west of the tracks, bush has taken over the site of the store and the blacksmith shop. Only a collapsing shell survives. The former Fitzgerald house, however, still stands and remains in use as a home.

The site of this ghost village lies on Foxmead Road about 3 km (1.8 miles) east of today's Foxmead.

GELERT

Until the 1850s the Haliburton Highlands remained inaccessible. Its small lakes and shallow rivers were its only highways. During that decade, to open this wilderness and to provide the influential lumber companies with food and labour, the government of Canada West laid out two dozen colonization roads, drawing settlers with offers of free land.

By 1860 the Bobcaygeon Colonization Road had been surveyed northward from the village of Bobcaygeon in the Kawartha Lakes region. Although much of the land through which it passed was rock and swamp, it did open up pockets of relatively fertile soil and these quickly sprouted hardworking pioneer communities.

Known during this period as Little Ireland, Gelert was located on a branch road that linked Kinmount on the Bobcaygeon Road with Haliburton on the Buckhorn Road. At first it was only a rural community with a sawmill, a church and a store.

The arrival of the Victoria Railway in 1878 changed all that. Overnight "Little Ireland" boomed into a busy shipping town and became known as Minden Station, after the nearby town. By 1895 it contained wool, shingle and saw mills as well as Methodist and Anglican churches. A side street was surveyed from the colonization road to the railway station and along it appeared Clark's blacksmith, Connor's hotel and Dawson's and Ritchie's general stores. Hartle and Levis operated a busy stage line shuttling passengers and

freight between Gelert and the growing mill town of Minden 8 km (5 miles) northwest on the Gull River. Most of the new arrivals were English, and the old name was quickly replaced with "Gelert."

Gelert's peak of prosperity was short-lived. The sandy soils, although productive at first, were quickly depleted. In the first decade of the last century alone, nearly two dozen farms were abandoned. Fires from careless lumbering razed what remained of the forests. The siding was lifted, and Gelert lost its economic mainstay, shipping.

For several years the store continued to serve a shrinking rural community and eventually even it closed down. Finally, in 1980, the CNR closed the little-used branch line completely.

Today Gelert is a semi-ghost town. Fewer than half its buildings are in permanent use; the rest lie vacant or are used only seasonally. The empty store and a handful of original houses and cabins line Cemetery Road, which leads east from County Road 1 to the site of the station. Here, where once stood station, sidings and cattle yards, there is now only a grassy meadow. Opposite the right of way, now a snowmobile trail, the cemetery remains well kept. A second store, being converted to a home, and the school, along with other early structures, line the county road itself.

The ghosts of Gelert lie along County Road 1 about 6 km (3.5 miles) east of Highway 121.

The former store is the most ghostly
relic in the partial ghost town of Gelert.

IRONDALE

In a remote and rugged part of Haliburton County, the iron-mining town of Irondale sputtered into existence amid a muddle of frustrating and futile mining ventures.

The first settlers to the area had been forced to pick their way along the new Monck Settlement Road, which was little better than a vague trail hacked through the dense woods. Some of the pioneers paused on the banks of Devil's Creek near the Irondale River to carve their farmsteads from the forest. Interest in the area began when W. Robinson struck iron while clearing his lot; shortly afterward, J. Campbell encountered a similar deposit.

Within a few short years a series of rag-tag mining ventures swung into action. The first iron deposits were quarried and hauled by wagon along the rugged Monck Road to the railway at nearby Kinmount. In 1881 an adventurous Irishman named Miles built a branch line from Kinmount seven miles to the iron deposit by the river. But after a few shipments, his resources were exhausted. Shortly afterward, two American investors, Parry and Mills, invested $200,000 on a smelting furnace, only to lose all in a disastrous fire.

In 1881 Charles Pusey and L.B. Howland formed the Toronto Iron Company and discovered further iron deposits. Their plans, the most ambitious to that date, entailed a labour force of 500 men and two blast furnaces that would turn out 22,000 tons of pig iron per year. Because local farmers were so busy cutting cordwood for the furnaces and tending to their clearings, Pusey and Howland were forced to import workers from Europe, particularly Italy, to quarry the ore and operate the smelter.

Long-time residents treated the mining prospects with some skepticism, as the *Minden Echo* of March 12, 1885, records: "The iron business is moving very slowly. As the 'inquisitive boy' would say, what is the reason? Because the men think they are working for a dead horse [as] they have worked for the same before. A former correspondence in the *Echo* says the miners were going to work with the company's old broken down engine; but unfortunately (or fortunately) they had to throw it out because it refused to do its work."

On the sandy banks of the river, the town of Irondale was surveyed and a brief boom followed. Miles' branch line was extended through the area to Bancroft and renamed the Irondale, Bancroft & Ottawa Railway. In addition to the company offices, boarding houses and miners' cottages, Irondale gained two general stores, which were operated by Charles J. Pusey and Peter Barr, an earlier settler. S.E. Hancock was the village blacksmith for many years and W. Checkey, the shoemaker. In 1889 Pusey added the beautiful white frame St. John the Baptist Church, which stands to this day.

The iron company operated until 1900, when the deposits finally ran out. As the mine closed and the workers migrated to greener pastures, the village's population slipped to fewer than 50. Many farmers were also forced to leave, as the miners had been the major market for their produce. Nonetheless, a small farm population lingered, surviving by shipping lumber on the new railway to mills at Kinmount and Gooderham, or outside the area. Barr's store and Hancock's smithy shop continued to operate for several years after the mine's demise.

In 1951 James Howland placed a tablet cast of iron from the old mine in the pretty church that Pusey had built, and dedicated it to his grandfather C.J. Pusey.

The photogenic little church stands in start contrast to the weedy rubble-strewn fields that once held Irondale's homes and businesses. The iron pit, on a rugged ridge overlooking the site, is filled with water. In 1960 the railway closed and the tracks were lifted (to be made into razor blades). While a number of the original village lots now sport newer homes, a pair of original houses stand on

The picturesque Pusey Church is the sole survivor in
Irondale's network of abandoned village streets.

Irondale Road east of the church. Many of the roads on
the town plot are now dead-end lanes or private driveways.

Little remains of the ghost Irondale, Bancroft &
Ottawa Railway. The right of way is visible only in a few
locales. A small flag station north of Kinmount remains at
the site of Howland Junction, the point where the IBO
railway joined the Victoria Railway. The best relic from

railway days is the Grand Trunk station, which still stands
in Kinmount and now serves as a seniors' drop-in centre.

The scenic landscape and the waters of nearby
Salerno Lake have attracted cottagers and, although the
halcyon days of the iron mining will never be repeated,
each summer brings with it a significant, if temporary,
burgeoning of Irondale's population.

MOWAT

On the shores of Canoe Lake, in Ontario's popular Algonquin Park, is the ghost town of Mowat complete, some say, with its own ghost.

By the 1880s, Ontario's logging companies were rapidly cutting into the lush pine stands of what is today "cottage country." In 1889, the Gilmour Company, having failed in a scheme to ship out logs via the Trent River system, established a mill on the north shore of Canoe Lake. The incentive for choosing that location was the arrival of a railway built by the now-legendary John Rudolphus Booth.

A short spur line (2.5 km/1.5 miles) linked the rail line with the mills on the lake, and by 1897 the noisy mill was in full swing. A village was created beside the mill and named in honour of Ontario's then premier, Oliver Mowat.

The village quickly grew to a population of more than 500, many of whom were workers living in the large two-storey bunkhouse. A few of the managers were accommodated in more commodious dwellings. At its peak Mowat would include a hospital, a cookhouse and warehouses, as well as farm buildings and a collection of shacks. A school was opened in 1898 to accommodate the estimated 100 children.

The first chapter in Mowat's life was surprisingly brief; in 1898 a depressed market for lumber silenced the mills. By 1900 the company was insolvent and by 1901 Mowat's population had plunged to two hundred.

By this time Algonquin Park was being heavily promoted by the Grand Trunk Railway, which had by then acquired Booth's railway line, and was beginning to attract tourists. In 1907 Shannon and Annie Fraser arrived, moving into the former Gilmour hospital. In 1913 they opened a hotel called Camp Mowat in what had been the company boarding house.

One of the hotel's frequent guests was painter Tom Thomson. In July of 1917 his body was found floating near the shore of the lake, his death a mystery. A wound on his head suggested that he may have fallen and drowned. Still, rumours and stories about murder involving a love triangle are still recounted. After Thomson was eventually buried near his home town of Leith, near Owen Sound, an apparition resembling his iconic grey canoe was reportedly seen floating on Canoe Lake, only to soon disappear.

Following a fire in 1920, the Frasers rebuilt Mowat Lodge. Their operation survived until 1930 when it too burned to the ground. Meanwhile, in 1926 the Canoe Lake Lumber Company opened a mill on Potter Creek, but it too closed in 1930. In 1939 Barry's Bay Lumber reactivated the Potter Creek mill but after a mere four years of operation it ceased operations. The school closed in the 1940s, and a small population remained in Mowat until the 1950s.

While tourists continued to arrive by train, few disembarked at the two-storey Canoe Lake station. Those who did would have remarked at the sign on the station which read: "Gentlemen will not, ladies do not, and others must not spit on the floor."

With the closing of an important bridge in 1933, through trains no longer called at Canoe Lake, although tourist trains continued to puff into the park until 1959. By then Highway 60, already open for nearly 20 years, offered the most popular access to the park.

Today, a few of the mill foundations can still be seen in overgrowth on the north west shore of Canoe Lake, where rotting timbers of the bridge to it protrude from the muddy waters of Potter Creek. On the north and west shores of the lake are some small cottages that had been homes in the Gilmour days. And high on a knoll accessible by a trail off a narrow sand track, a tiny cemetery still shelters the grave markers of the three individuals to be buried there.

The site is accessible from the Canoe Lake Store by canoe or small motorboat. If you see a grey canoe with no one in it, don't blink or it may be gone.

Following the demise of the sawmills, Mowat gained new life as a tourist destination, the Gilmour boarding house becoming Mowat Lodge.

Lumber king John Rudolphus Booth inspects a shipment of pine. Booth built the rail line that gave rise to the mills at Mowat.

The collapsing schoolhouse is the
only building left in the once-thriving
Nipissing Road village of Rye.

RYE

The Nipissing Colonization Road was another of those pioneer settlement roads to which hopeful settlers flocked in large numbers when the lumber camps were in operation, but which they soon fled in equal numbers when the soil proved useless for farming. Several stagecoach stopping places appeared along the route, most of which have vanished with little trace. Farms are overgrown, their barns collapsed shells.

South of Magnetawan, the only village of any size, the road is passable year-round; north of that point it becomes little more than a track through the woods.

Near a pocket of farmland 19 km (12 miles) north of Magnetawan, the road re-emerges from the forest at the former stopping places of Rye and Mecunoma. At Mecunoma stood a two-storey hotel with the interesting name of "Bummer's Roost"; it was built in 1882 and burned in 1926. Local lore suggests the hotel earned its nickname from a local ne'er-do-well named Dick the Bummer. Its actual name was the Russell House and it was said to have predated the hotels at Magnetawan. A newer home has since arisen on the old foundations, while a historical plaque on the road recounts the site's colourful history.

A short distance east of Bummer's Roost, at the corner of the Eagle Lake Road and the Rye Road, an ancient wooden house with a two-storey porch is the former Deer Lake Lodge, now a privately owned residence.

Five kilometres (3 miles) north of the lodge on the Rye Road is the site of the one-time village of Rye, named after a town in southeast England. At its peak it boasted four hotels, a school and an evangelical church. A post office operated out of a succession of private homes until 1964. As there were a few farms nearby, Rye likely contained a store and blacksmith shop as well, but no records of these have remained, either on paper or in local recollection. A small mica mine operated briefly near the school, but it produced no usable quantities of the glassy substance.

Today Rye is totally deserted, a victim of a mass exodus to the prairies. The collapsed and decaying hotel and the vacant buildings became curiosities for the children of nearby summer camps, but all evidence of these has vanished. The church stood until the 1980s when it was dismantled, leaving only the Rye Cemetery. The school remains, abandoned, collapsing and almost completely hidden behind bushes and small trees. A couple of one-time farms still stand on the Rye Road near the village.

Much of the young forest has in recent years been logged, leaving behind little evidence not only of the village but also little of the forest cover that would have greeted the earliest inhabitants of Rye.

North of Rye the Nipissing Road has for several kilometres been totally reclaimed by the forest. The next village north of Rye is Commanda. It contains one of Ontario's most elaborately built and best-preserved country stores. It is now the site of a tea room, gift shop and museum.

The Rye Road can be found by following the Eagle Lake Road west from the village of South River on Highway 11.

Despite its location on the rugged remains of the Nipissing Road, the cemetery in the vanished village of Rye continues to be well kept.

SCOTIA JUNCTION

Soon after the Muskoka Colonization Road opened up the northern sections of Muskoka and eastern Parry Sound to settlers, the railways began their influx. In 1888, the Northern Pacific Junction line was extended north from Gravenhurst to North Bay, and stations placed at Emsdale, Novar and Scotia. A small settlement sprang up around the Scotia station and included a hotel, general store, blacksmith, church and school.

In 1894, J.R. Booth launched his railway empire by building his Ottawa, Arnprior & Parry Sound Railway from Ottawa to Depot Harbour on Georgian Bay. His route crossed that of the Grand Trunk at Scotia, and the village was renamed Scotia Junction.

More railway facilities were needed. Yards were laid out and switching tracks laid down. The station where the lines crossed was a two-tone wooden depot with a decorative tower at the corner. Additional facilities were also needed for crews, and for passengers who were changing trains to head into Algonquin Park. Soon the streets contained three hotels, boarding houses, and homes for the railway crews. The Albinson Hotel was said to have stood three storeys high.

In 1912 the pretty little towered station burned and was replaced with a simpler single-storey structure. By 1923, both routes were in the hands of the financially troubled Grand Trunk Railway and became part of the Canadian National Railway system. So too did the Canadian Northern Railway, which by then was offering a more direct route to Depot Harbour through Parry Sound itself. The yards at Scotia Junction were closed and employees let go. The village slipped into a decline. In 1933 the line through Algonquin Park was severed by a damaged bridge, and eastbound trains went no further than the Highland Inn in the park.

Although rail traffic continued to flow west to Depot Harbour, that too dwindled and stopped altogether when the grain elevators burned in 1945. Today, little remains of the once-busy rail junction. Only a solitary boarding house still stands, currently as a private home. The main street now contains only a pair of silent stores and rubble-strewn fields. The yards and track junction are no longer visible, having been reclaimed by a marsh. Throughout the further reaches of the townsite, a few newer homes have been added to soften the ghostly landscape that is Scotia Junction.

The near-empty village is located on Station Road between Highway 11 and Highway 592 about 3 km (1.8 miles) south of Emsdale. The remaining single track is still used by CN freights and the Ontario Northland's popular *Northlander* passenger train, which links Toronto, North Bay and Cochrane.

Businesses on Scotia Junction's main street have all closed.

Of the many sidings and boarding houses in the noisy railway town of Scotia Junction, only one former boarding house stands by a single track.

A wooden bridge carries Nipissing Road traffic to the ghost town of Seguin Falls.

Seguin Falls' small flag stop station disappeared during the 1940s when the trains stopped calling.

SEGUIN FALLS

As a ghost town, Seguin Falls first came to light in one of Harvey Currell's *Toronto Telegram* travel columns as a "ghost town worth visiting." In 1873 the village, located about a day's stagecoach ride north from Ashdown, consisted of little more than a hotel, sawmill and post office. Soon the reputation of the hotel spread, causing a contemporary traveller to comment in 1885: "The traveller will find an excellent temperance hotel at Seguin Falls, the proprietor of which, Mr. D.F. Burk, is a most genial and hospitable host, nor should we forget to praise the excellent cuisine of his good lady."

The village also included Adam Fitzer's store and blacksmith shop as well as a church and school, all clustered about the junction of the Nipissing Road with the Christie Settlement Road.

In 1897 J.R. Booth's railway arrived and a small flag stop station was built about 8 km (5 miles) south of the hamlet where the Spence Lumber Company established a new sawmill. The older hotel closed and a new hotel, the King George, opened beside the station. William Fry, W.S. Morrison and Julius Pearlman all opened general stores, and a string of dwellings appeared. While the grander homes of the village's wealthier residents nestled amid the shady maples south of the station, north of the station, on a bare rocky ridge, the workers' simple cabins straggled along the road. Here too stood Methodist and Anglican churches, while a new brick school was built in 1922. The village possessed no street pattern, the Nipissing Road being its main and only thoroughfare.

Long after the importance of the Nipissing Colonization Road had declined, Seguin Falls continued to thrive as a major lumber-shipping station. Through traffic on Booth's line, then operated by Canadian National, ended in 1933, however, when a bridge was damaged in Algonquin Park and CN failed to find the funds to repair it. After that, the rails ended at Scotia Junction on CN's Toronto-North Bay line, and fewer trains came to call.

Nevertheless, Mrs. Thomas MacKinnon operated the hotel and confectionery well into the 1950s. But the farm population of Montieth Township, in which Seguin Falls was located, dwindled from 480 in 1921 to a mere 50 in 1961. Then, in 1955, when the railway closed, the village's residents began to move away. By 1960 Seguin Falls' many buildings, save two, stood vacant. The empty church retained its altar cloth and hymnals but no longer heard the voices of worship. Both churches are gone now, and the handsome hotel burned in 1988. A number of newer homes now occupy the sites of the earlier stores and cabins, while the two-storey Vigras house has been extensively renovated. During the winter, Booth's right of way roars back to life as a path for the Seguin Snowmobile Trail.

Although abandoned buildings are few, the silence and the remoteness evoke the "ghosts" of a busier era. It's still a "ghost town worth visiting."

SOUTH PORTAGE

By 1868 much of Muskoka had been opened up, thanks to the Muskoka Colonization Road and its network of sideroads. After the Brunel Road had been cut from the Muskoka Road to Mary Lake at Port Sydney, work began on a canal that would allow navigation along the Muskoka River into Fairy Lake and Peninsula Lake. But a stubborn height of land obstructed the final connection from Peninsula Lake to the all-important Lake of Bays, where logging remained vital and tourism lay on the horizon.

In 1895 a charter was granted to allow steamboat operations on Lake of Bays and an electric tramway to link it with Peninsula Lake. In 1902 the charter was changed to allow for the construction of hotels, docks and boarding houses as well. In addition, the electric tram would be a steam train operation.

In 1905 the train's first run took place. The coaches at first consisted of four horse-drawn streetcars formerly owned by the Toronto Street Railway, which were joined to form two railway coaches. Two 20-foot boxcars were built to accommodate the movement of freight. They were hauled over the portage by a pair of four-wheeled saddle tank steam engines.

The village of South Portage developed at the portage's base of operation on the shore of Lake of Bays. Although a few buildings had already stood here when the portage was a wagon road, the railway required engine houses, docks, hotels, boarding houses and homes for the employees. Most of the structures were clustered around the engine shed and the passenger shed at the end of the portage. A bit further east a grid network of streets was laid out, where additional buildings were located.

For its first few decades, the little line served the needs of hotels and logging camps by hauling freight as well as passengers. During the 1950s, however, the auto age brought paved roads and individual cottages. Gone were the days of steamships taking vacationers to resorts. By 1960 most of the steamships had been retired and the portage railway ran for the last time.

The village of South Portage too began to decline. From being a busy terminus for trains and steamers, it became almost a ghost town. A new dock has obliterated the site of the engine shed and the passenger dock. The many buildings near the wharf disappeared with new road construction. The network of streets east of the new dock now contains a dwindling number of the early buildings, some in ruin, others used only seasonally. The South Portage marina is the only reminder of the community's busier times.

The story has an upbeat ending, however. Thanks to a decade of work by dedicated volunteers, the equipment from the railway has been reassembled beside the Muskoka Heritage Place pioneer village in Huntsville and now carries tourists from its new station along the banks of the Muskoka River to a 1909 purser's cabin from Norway Point, which serves as the railway's Fairy Lake station.

South Portage is situated on South Portage Road a short distance south of Highway 60.

Much of what was the village of South Portage is gradually succumbing to rot and weather.

The engine and baggage car of the *Portage Flyer* at its southern terminus of South Portage.

125

The old general store in Swords lends a picturesquely ghostly presence.

A rusting sign on Swords' old general store once attracted shoppers. Now it attracts only photographers and ghost-towners.

SWORDS

First called Maple Lake Station, Swords began as a siding for the Ludgate Lumber Company, which built a mill, a store and several houses for its mill workers. John Swords' Maple Lake Hotel had become the destination for a particular group of American tourists calling themselves the American Flyers, who journeyed by train each summer to Swords' popular hotel. In 1904 a school was added to the village. When Swords took over the general store as well, the name was changed to reflect the influence of the village's leading business owners.

By the 1930s the tourist trains and the lumbering had both ended. The station was removed in 1946, while the store closed 20 years after that. As in Seguin Falls, Swords' townsfolk moved away. However, the lush fields kept farmers longer. And then, in the 1950s, the cottage boom struck, followed, in the 1970s, by a boom in country living. Since then, the Maple Lake area has grown into a busy community of cottagers and Parry Sound commuters.

Surrounded as it now is by farm fields and comfortable country homes, the ghost town of Swords seems oddly out of place. South of the former railway roadbed, which is now part of the Seguin Snowmobile Trail, the weathered two-storey hotel is now only partially used as a residence, while the attached store stands disused. Its rusting signs and dusty storefront windows give the old store the authentic feel of being in a ghost town. The workers' cabins that had been south of the store on the same side of the road, are gone now, either to be renovated or replaced by newer homes. The school, further south, has been renovated into a community centre.

Swords lies 3.5 km (2 miles) south of Highway 587, on the Swords Road, about 3 km (1.8 miles) west of Orrville.

Old doors mark the former hotel in Swords, to which the abandoned general store is attached.

Uffington's former schoolhouse
has been converted into a home.

UFFINGTON

As colonization roads began to penetrate the forests of Muskoka, settlers moved in to take up their land. During the 1880s and 1890s, as farmers cleared the land around Uffington, lumbermen stripped away the tall pine forests. Here, Robert McMurray made his way along the Peterson Colonization Road, and, a short distance east of the Muskoka Colonization Road, opened up a general store. His nearest rival, a mile or so to the east, was George Spence, who added a second store.

Uffington developed around the two locations with three churches: Anglican, Presbyterian and Methodist, the two-and-a-half storey Peterkin Hotel, a blacksmith shop and several private homes. The growing community could also claim an agricultural society and a township hall. However, the nearest mills were several kilometres north of Uffington at Mathiasville on the Muskoka River.

As throughout the district of Muskoka, the soil around Uffington was sandy and stoney – generally discouraging for farmers. Many followed the trek to the wheatfields of the west, and Uffington began to fade.

Most village functions have disappeared – the stores have closed, two of the three churches are silent and the blacksmith shop has long vanished. Several early village houses still cluster around the two intersections; in their midst a number of newer homes have been added to the landscape. The fields along Uffington's concession roads have become overgrown and barns have collapsed, while most of the old farm homes have been replaced by modern country dwellings.

The western portion of the village includes the large two-storey former hotel, McMurray's former general store, and the vague foundations of the blacksmith shop. St. Paul's Anglican Church, closer to the eastern end of the village, still functions, while at the eastern crossroads four original village homes, although weathered, still remain seasonally occupied. Across the road from the cemetery, south of the intersection, the one-time Methodist church sits vacant and showing the effects of time.

The westernmost of Uffington's two village clusters lies at the intersection of Hawn Road and Peterson Road about 2 km (1.2 miles) south of Regional Road 118, while Muskoka Road 20 contains the eastern cluster of village buildings.

Uffington's Anglican church still sees worship service.

UHTHOFF

With the opening of the Midland Railway from Orillia to Midland in 1875, mill operators found the railways a convenient means of shipping lumber, and built their mills right at trackside. Uhthoff was one such place.

Named after a place in Germany, Uhthoff opened its first post office in 1880 and included the lumber mill, a blacksmith shop, a United Methodist church, an Orange Hall, a small railway station, a store and half a dozen homes, all situated on the east side of Uhthoff Line.

After the first store was destroyed in 1943 by fire, a conflagration that consumed several buildings, the village remained without a store until 1949. With increasing competition from stores in New Uhthoff a few kilometres away and from Orillia, the store lasted only 10 more years.

Following the closing of the mills, a new operation came upon the scene. In 1905 the limestone deposits that lay near the surface began to attract quarry operations. In 1911 the CPR opened a line close to the quarries and named their station Uhthoff. The village of New Uhthoff grew near here as well.

As the quarry operations expanded, the life of old Uhthoff was prolonged. But finally, in 1968, the quarry began to intrude on the village itself, and the buildings were removed. The old Grand Trunk station, the first to go, was removed in 1968 (the Grand Trunk had taken over the Midland Railway in 1882). The last was a private house, one of the village's largest, in 1981.

The Grand Trunk tracks were lifted shortly after that, as were those of the CPR, the latter becoming a hiking trail. While the quarries continue to operate, little survives of the ghost town.

The remains that exist lie on Fairgrounds Road just south of Thorburn Road and about 15 km (9 miles) north of Orillia. These consist of vague cellar holes, the foundations and steps from the Orange Hall, and a path through a field that formerly lead to the once-busy railway station.

The road that led to Uhthoff's railway station is now merely a track in a field.

The foundations of Uhthoff's Orange
Lodge are now heavily overgrown.

The fishing port and railway town of Jackfish thrived for six decades before becoming a ghost town. *(Library and Archives Canada)*

CHAPTER 4

TRAILS TO THE
NORTH

BURCHELL LAKE

GOLD ROCK

BERENS RIVER

Thunder Bay

SILVER ISLET

Lake Superior

H 17

JACKFISH

GARGANTUA

GOUDREAU

Sault Ste. Marie

LOCHALSH

COCKBURN ISLAND

DALTON

NICHOLSON

NESTERVILLE

Chapleau

H 129

H 17

BISCOTASING

VICTORIA MINES

MICHAEL'S BAY

BENNY

H 144

CREIGHTON

Sudbury

MILNET

FRENCH RIVER

H 69

PICKEREL LANDING

DESAULNIERS

PAKESLEY

North Bay

H 11

SILVER CENTRE

KIOSK

(not to scale)

An abandoned cabin stands guard
precariously in Benny.

BENNY

Benny sprang to life around 1880 as Pulp Siding, a shipping point for the Spanish, Strong and Hope Lumber companies. Two dozen cabins, three boarding houses, a church, a store and a poolroom clustered around the CPR station. The sidings were piled with pulpwood awaiting shipment.

Pulp Siding briefly fell silent in 1911 when the mills shut down, but gained new life just two years later when the Spanish Pulp and Paper Company began logging on a nearby lake. At this time the name was changed to Benny to honour an engineer on the railway.

The town grew to a reported 700 residents with a new school, a hotel and a Roman Catholic church. During this time, the only access to the town was by rail (a 15-cent train ride from Sudbury), with a solitary phone line its only other link. Benny's baseball team competed in a small league that included neighbouring railway communities like Levack and Cartier. If they celebrated their victories too vigorously, rowdies might find themselves in the converted cattle car that served as the local lockup … as might the moonshiners who supplied them.

Then in 1928, two years after it took over the mill,

the Hope Lumber Company shut down its operations. During the road construction programs of the Depression, Benny gained road access to the larger CPR divisional town of Cartier, and many of the residents moved out. Others found work on the government roads, some served as guides for American hunters, and a few others found work in the newly opened Geneva Mine, although it too shut down in 1944.

The vacant mill burned in 1943, and the school and post office closed a decade later. Benny's residents by then numbered a mere two dozen.

Four surviving cabins are still occupied near the track, while the ground where the rest of the town stood is vacant. A few new homes have been added to the periphery of the townsite following the opening of Highway 144. Overgrown fields still show signs of the sidings where rail cars once burst with pulp logs. The CPR's portable prefabricated aluminum station now sits silent too and VIA Rail trains slip by without stopping.

To reach Benny, watch for the sign beside Highway 144, pointing west down a dirt road about 8 km (5 miles) north of Cartier.

Few of Benny's trackside buildings are still around.

The Berens River headframe saw
much gold hauled from its shafts.

BERENS RIVER

Deep in the remote, nearly inaccessible tamarack forests of far northwestern Ontario is an incongruous sight: a bowling alley and a swimming pool. Nearby are the bunkhouses and homes that 60 years ago were home to 600 people. Today they survive, altered only by the vagaries of nature, as one of Ontario's most complete ghost towns. And that is largely because Berens River is one of its least known and least accessible.

In 1935 gold fever raced across Ontario's northland. Prospectors and mining magnates walked, paddled or flew to the glittering distant strikes. To tap one gold find near Ontario's sub-arctic border with Manitoba, H. Dewitt Smith formed the Newmount Mining Company. Throughout 1936, small planes chugged over the treetops carrying men, machines and furniture and by January, 1937, Smith had in place his mine buildings, a pair of bunkhouses, a dining hall, an office and his executive quarters.

The cost of air transport was prohibitive even then, and Smith began to slash a road through the tamaracks from Berens River Landing on Lake Winnipeg. In 1940 he added a five-bed hospital, more bunkhouses and a sawmill. By then he had taken from the ground 5,800 ounces of gold and 177,000 ounces of silver.

Berens River quickly grew from a mere mining camp into a self-sufficient town. In 1941 Smith spent $23,900 to build an apartment building, $5,600 for a school and $3,200 for a police station with what is arguably North America's smallest jail, an outhouse-sized concrete cubicle with a single door and tiny barred window.

The falls on a nearby river powered the community's own hydro plant. Then, to encourage employees to build homes in the town site, Smith provided each with an interest-free loan of $800.

By 1942 the workforce numbered 210, within an overall population of 600. Remoteness from road and rail links, and a lack of scheduled commercial air service, made Berens River Ontario's most isolated non-native settlement. To offset the remoteness and restlessness, Smith provided a recreation hall with a swimming pool and a bowling alley.

Arctic-like winters that were long and cold meant a compact townsite was needed. While the bunkhouses and recreation facilities huddled close to the mine buildings, the houses lined curved "streets" on an adjacent hilltop.

During the war, the defence department removed gold mining from the list of protected war industries, and miners from across the country left the mines to enlist. By 1945, when the war ended and metal prices fell, Smith's workforce numbered just 164. Production continued to decline for three more years until August 31, 1948, when Smith dismantled the plant and said farewell to his employees.

With nowhere to move the buildings, few vandals to cause damage and a climate that is dry and cold, Berens River remains much as it was left on that August day. Except for a few mine buildings that were dismantled, the town, with houses and hospital, bowling alley and swimming pool, still sits silently in the northern woods.

Today as then, the only access is by chartered plane. It lies near the south shore of South Trout Lake. A topographical map and aerial photos will be needed.

This log cabin once housed a goldminer's family in Berens River.

BISCOTASING

Biscotasing began its colourful existence in 1880 as a base for CPR construction crews then laying the route of Canada's first national rail line. For the next six years, Bisco, as it was known, was a divisional point for the growing CPR, with 15 engineers, three telegraphers, sidings, a wye for turning locomotives around, a watering tower and coal docks. Train crews and station staff called drafty boarding houses home. A nearby mill cut ties for the track laying. After the tracks reached Chapleau in 1886, the divisional facilities were relocated to the new town, and Biscso's growth slowed.

The rail line opened new stands of timber, however, and in 1894 two sawmills began operation. In 1891 Booth and Shannon, one of Canada's largest timber producers, assumed the mills, and Bisco's economy accelerated. By 1911 the mill was grinding out more than 14 million board feet of lumber. The town added a school, a new general store and two churches, one Anglican, the other Catholic. Thirty new homes brought Bisco's population to nearly 300. The CPR replaced its earlier station with a new two-storey depot.

As with many northern mill towns, fire was an ever-present danger. One of the worst raced through the town in 1912, destroying the mill and many of the town structures. But the mill and most of the town were rebuilt. In 1923, with much of the timber gone, the mill changed hands. It struggled on until 1929, when it closed for good.

By the following year Bisco's population had dropped from 250 to a mere 7. Despite a resurgence in the 1950s when the E.B. Eddie Company began logging the area, the town's year-round population remains at only 20, a figure that rises considerably during the summer season.

Despite its faded glory, Bisco was once home to a strange and controversial character. Long fascinated by Canada's wilderness, and in particular its native peoples, an Englishman named Archibald Belaney moved to Bisco in 1912 and befriended its native community, marrying one of its members as his first wife. After a rowdy residency in the town, Belaney disappeared.

A few years later a tall, hawk-nosed figure wearing fringed leather and braids appeared from the Canadian woods. Calling himself Chief Grey Owl, he rapidly gained fame as a lecturer and writer of wildlife conservation and has long been credited with having saved the Canadian beaver from extinction. Years later, after Grey Owl had died in his remote Saskatchewan cabin, an astonished world learned that Grey Owl had not been an Indian after all, but an Englishman named Archibald Belaney. Today photographs of Belaney decorate the walls of the store, while his name is used by a nearby resort.

Grey Owl would recognize only portions of today's Biscotasing, however. While the Anglican church and the general store still function, many of the original cabins are used only seasonally by hunters and fishers. Most of the surviving structures are well maintained, and indeed many are being replaced by newer cottages. The most complete street of original houses lies to the west of the railway tracks where the abandoned Catholic church clings to a rocky hilltop.

Regrettably, the CPR removed its handsome station in the 1990s. It was replaced by a shelter, where VIA Rail's Sudbury to White River train service still calls three times a week in each direction.

While rail remains the most comfortable way to reach Biscotasing, it is possible to drive in. From Highway 144, 96 km (60 miles) north of Cartier, the Ramsay Road leads west for 38 km (23.5 miles) to the Biscotasing turn-off. From there, a 37 km (23 mile) winding road leads ultimately to the waters of Biscotasi Lake and the weathered buildings of the partial ghost town on its shore. Both roads are gravel and the going is often rough.

Biscotasing's most famous personality was Archie "Grey Owl" Belaney (seated, right), an Englishman who fooled thousands into thinking he was a native Indian.

The old Catholic church sits weathered atop its rocky perch overlooking the partial ghost town of Biscotasing.

These log dwellings were the first houses constructed in the mining town of Burchell Lake.

Abandoned for 40 years, the bungalows of Burchell Lake are now engulfed by bush.

BURCHELL LAKE

In 1876 three prospectors named McNaughton, McMillan and McFee were the first to discover copper on the shores of Burchell Lake, some 160 km (100 miles) west of Thunder Bay. It was not until 1901, however, when the Ontario & Rainy River Branch of the Canadian Northern Railway finally breached the area, that production could begin. In that year, with a workforce of just 14, the Tip Top Mine produced 768,000 pounds of copper worth $30,700. The town consisted then only of a simple office and, near the shores of the placid Burchell Lake a kilometre away, several log dwellings. Falling copper prices, however, soon forced the mine to close.

During the Great War, copper prices rebounded and re-ignited interest in the property. A narrow-gauge railway siding was built, and for two years the mine churned out 45 tons of ore per day. But the rejuvenation was short-lived. After the war ended, copper prices tumbled again and Tip Top fell silent.

The years following the Second World War, however, would be the boom years for Burchell Lake. In 1956 Coldstream Copper Mines constructed a 1,000-ton concentrator, and in 1959 L.R. Redford and G.H. MacDonald added a new electric pump. They also laid out an elaborate townsite that they named Burchell Lake.

By the lake, on the old village site, Redford and MacDonald constructed 11 log homes of special double-tongued British Columbia cedar for management. Their floors were polished hardwood, their ceilings open-beamed.

In the shadow of the concentrator on curved suburban-like streets, they added 24 modest, but modern bungalows and 17 mobile homes. Beside the mine gate were four bunkhouses and a BA gas station. A pump house and lagoon provided water and sewage facilities, while mercury vapour lights kept the site bright. Residents could curl, play baseball or challenge their rivals in nearby lumber towns to hockey on their own rink – or they could simply shoot pool in Kaski's general store. A two-room school provided education for the town's children. At its peak, the community would number 400 residents.

In just five years the mine yielded copper, gold and silver worth $28 million. But on August 5, 1966, a depressed market again forced the mine to close and the residents left. The mine buildings survived for a few years, but were later removed. New workings in the late 1990s failed to revive mine operations, and today nothing remains of the mine buildings. While the trailers too are gone, and the bunkhouses and store are demolished, much of the remaining town sits intact. A growing forest has obscured many of the buildings whose simple forms yet linger. The bungalows still line the curving streets, their yards now heavily overgrown. Rusting fire hydrants hide in the tall grass, while beside the school young trees push through the mesh of the baseball cage. The old gas station still stands too, although it is difficult to make it out through the bush. The lovely former managers' cedar houses by the lake are now used as summer camps.

The townsite sits behind a protective chain link gate at the end of what was provincial Highway 802, south of Highway 11-71.

COCKBURN ISLAND

In the 1870s the land rush to Manitoulin Island was in full swing. Many of those settlers squatted on Cockburn Island, a 6,500 hectare (25 square mile) limestone outcrop situated 4 km (2.5 miles) from Manitoulin's western tip. Thanks largely to its timber potential, Cockburn Island's population quickly reached 1,000. Cockburn Island at its peak contained two school districts, a community of farmers and four villages, the largest of which would be Tolsmaville.

One of the earliest arrivals was a fisherman from Michigan named Zeb Tolsma. In the island's only natural harbour, he established a fishing operation with a store, a boarding house and several cabins. The community adopted his name and became known as Tolsmaville. By 1883 the village contained 17 buildings, and the island soon became a self-governing township with Tolsmaville as its administrative and social centre.

From his base on Cockburn Island, Tolsma could access the bountiful fishing grounds of the North Channel, which lay between the island and the mainland. From his secondary base on the Duck Islands, further east, he could troll the banks just off Manitoulin Island itself. Then in 1884, Tolsma strangely vanished. Whether he drowned in a storm or fled to escape an unknown threat is a mystery that has yet to be solved.

Tolsmaville was not the island's only settlement, however. The island's surveyor, J.W. Fitzgerald, had enticingly written: "With the exception of a narrow belt around the southwest and north shore, the whole interior is fairly suited for agriculture." Following his assessment, the Indian band that owned the land agreed to sell the land to settlers for 50 cents an acre, keeping for themselves a small reserve on the northwestern portion of the island. Soon, arriving steamers began to unload settlers eager to take up their new lots. In 1881 the township was incorporated and elected its first reeve and council.

Four kilometres south of Tolsmaville, a small group of Scottish pioneers began to carve out the island's first farm. Led by the Goodmurphies, McLeods, Reids and Houghts, the "Scotch Block" formed the heart of the farming community across the centre of the island. Farming boomed, and within 20 years more than 40 farms lined the island's four concession roads.

On the western end of the island, the local First Nations band, which had turned over much of the island to the settlers, retained a small reserve and the village of Jabaiansing, which contained a small school and a Catholic church. The band's Anglican members attended the church in Tolsmaville. Following an acrimonious split between the band's two religions, the Anglicans moved to a larger reserve on Manitoulin Island. The remaining members gradually relocated as well, leaving Jabaiansing a ghost village.

On the island's south shore, a small village grew up around a sawmill and took the name Ricketts Harbour. Here, the Lawson brothers of Owen Sound built a saw- and shingle mill. The village also contained a store, an Anglican mission chapel, a boarding house and a string of small cabins for the workers. Nearby, the Olmsteds operated a fishing station, and for several years the little cove buzzed with the coming and going of fishing and lumber tugs. The station vanished when the mill ceased operation.

For 40 years Cockburn Island prospered. Fishermen and farmers swelled the population to over 300, and when loggers crowded into the boarding houses during the peak of the lumbering season, the population often exceeded 1,000. The years following the First World War saw the island's first setbacks. Returning veterans sought better jobs and brighter lights in Ontario's towns and cities. Overfishing and the sea lamprey would later combine to devastate the fishery, and the last commercial fishing operation ended in 1944. By 1947 small-scale lumbering was also finished.

This left Tolsmaville as the only occupied community on the island. And even here, after the end of the Second World War, residents began to move to the mainland. Farming was no longer economical, much of the timber had gone, and better schools and opportunities awaited in places like Blind River and Sault Ste. Marie. Finally, in 1963, the CPR discontinued its steamer service to the island, and Tolsmaville became a ghost town too. Astonishingly, it retained its municipal status and continued to elect a reeve and council even though its permanent population stood at just three.

Although the long-time residents have moved away, many have retained their island properties. For this reason, many of Tolsmaville's early buildings have survived. On the main street, the store, the school and the church, with its small graveyard, are maintained. Side streets still contain many of the simple frame houses that islanders called home just five decades ago. Recently, newer cottages and summer homes have appeared around the little harbour.

Outside the village, farm roads have deteriorated into narrow lanes through a dark forest of plantation pines, many of which are being newly logged. The Indian village on the far western end of the island has been completely vacated.

In 1999 the Ontario government announced funds to help upgrade the island's facilities to include a public park along the beach with washroom facilities and a storage building. The township has also upgraded communications between the island and the mainland with the installation of a two-line radio-telephone system.

To reach Cockburn Island, it is necessary to travel either to Thessalon or to Meldrum Bay on Manitoulin Island and make private arrangements with a boat owner.

The former Tolsmaville schoolhouse is still well kept, although the village no longer has permanent residents.

CREIGHTON

Although the region west of Sudbury harboured a well-known deposit of iron, mining did not become economical until 1883 when the CPR built its Algoma Eastern Railway into the area. In that year the Canada Copper Company – today's INCO – acquired the property and it began shipping ore in 1901. Its remoteness required a townsite and so a community was established. The post office opened in 1902, and a school in 1904. A Roman Catholic church was added in 1916. A main street lined the tracks where a two-storey station stood. The townsite would soon claim 900 residents.

The town continued to grow until its population reached a peak of 2,000 in 1964. Among its businesses were a Bank of Toronto, an IGA grocery store and the Rio movie theatre. Over the years, the town enjoyed a wide range of business operations, including a tailor, a hairdresser and a laundry, as well as a billiard hall, a barber and a butcher. More than 400 family homes lined the community's winding streets, while single miners could live in one of the town's four boarding houses.

Although the mine continued operations, the town's population began to dwindle and by the early 1980s was down to 800. With road improvements, and employment opportunities in nearby Sudbury, many people moved out, and a number of the more dilapidated neighbourhoods were cleared of their buildings.

Then, in 1986, INCO announced to the shocked villagers that it would close ... not just the mine but the very town itself. Underground water and sewer services had lain so long neglected that costs of repair had become prohibitive. Even the nearest local municipality shunned the prospect of assuming such a liability.

Creighton's fate was sealed. By 1988 most of its residents had gone. The bulldozers moved in and in less than a year had left only foundations and dusty roads to remind the visitor that here had stood one of the north's largest and oldest company mining towns.

The site of Creighton lies on Regional Road 24, a short distance east of Highway 144. At the intersection on the way to the mine, a small commemorative park contains a cairn and a heritage plaque that depicts the layout of the town during its heyday, along with a list of its former businesses. The road continues to the mine entrance, where the tracks have been removed. Here, where the main street once bustled with activity, the old roads have been blocked off to vehicles, although the sidewalks and the foundations can still be discerned in the growing vegetation.

In 1999 Creighton made the headlines for a wildly different reason. Due to the unusual depth of its shaft (2000 m/6,800 feet), the mine in 1999 became the site of the Sudbury Neutrino Observatory to detect the passing of the infinitesimally small neutrino particles that emanate from the sun.

An overview of the mining town of Creighton before the residents were ordered out.

The main street sits devoid of all structures two years after INCO ended the mining town's 80-year existence.

A view of the first station at Dalton. *(CP Archives)*

A handful of buildings linger tennously on Dalton's track-side streets.

DALTON MILLS/DALTON STATION

One of the most prolific lumber empires in north-eastern Ontario was that of Austin and Nicholson. By the 1920s its first mill town, Nicholson, located near Chapleau, was basking in its heyday and the Austin-Nicholson empire was expanding. The growth led to an additional mill and a new town named Dalton Mills. With an unprecedented 1,000 hectare (2,460-acre) townsite, it was to be located on the Shakwamka River where a flat sandy peninsula proved an ideal construction site.

Here, in 1921, the company built the most advanced mill of the day. "The equipment of the mill is in every way modern," observed the *Canadian Lumberman and Woodworker* in October, 1922. "Much of the heavy work is done away with. The transferring of ties or lumber is all done by foot pedals." At first Dalton Mills claimed only six dwellings and two bunkhouses, but within two years it had boomed into a flourishing town. While the town itself covered the west bank of the river, the mill and its buildings lay across the wooden bridge on the eastern bank.

Dalton Mills provided workers with facilities unheard of in Ontario's other rugged lumber camps. Besides indoor toilets and electricity, the lumbermen enjoyed two lanes of bowling, five pool tables, an ice cream parlour and a movie theatre. In the Plaza Theatre, wrote the *Canadian Lumberman and Woodworker*, "there was always a full house and there was always a rush for the ice cream parlour after the show." Clearly Dalton Mills was no average lumber camp. By 1923 it boasted two churches, a store and 36 houses. The two-storey bunkhouse contained 100 bedrooms, each complete with bed, table, bench and spittoon. A butcher shop with a freezer kept the town supplied with fresh meat. By 1927 more than 80 buildings clustered on the two riverbanks, ranking Dalton Mills among the largest towns in northeastern Ontario.

Five kilometres (3 miles) north at Dalton Station on the CPR main line lay the Austin loading yards. The station, railway section house and a handful of houses became the focus for the next phase of Dalton Mills' lumbering history.

Dalton Mills survived its first mill fire in 1939, but when the mill burned again in 1949 the Austin Lumber Company (Nicholson had retired in 1934) abandoned the site. A newer mill at Bertrand, 90 km (55 miles) west, satisfied all demand. Austin's license of occupation dictated that all buildings be removed from the site and in short order homes were burnt, moved or simply collapsed into a ghostly rubble.

In 1956 the W. Plaunt Company of Sudbury purchased the Austin Company and in 1962 it opened a new electric mill at Dalton Station. For a time the new Dalton was as busy as the old. Its station, church, school, mill, gas station and dozen homes lined a network of dirt streets beside the track. But fire again destroyed the mill in 1979 and halted the town's growth for a third and final time.

The scars are still fresh. Half a dozen buildings, some abandoned, including the former Catholic church which is now used as a seasonal residence, line the old network of streets. Meanwhile, time and the forest have claimed most of old Dalton Mills. The bridge cribbing still crosses the river narrows, while two houses, including the former Austin house, survive as cottages. Other than these, the cemetery and rotting timbers are all that remain. The Daltons lie on Highway 651, 27 km (17 miles) north of Highway 129, and 75 km (46 miles) west of Chapleau.

The former hotel in the railside community
of Desaulniers looks out over a now-quiet
street that once led to the station.

DESAULNIERS

Desaulniers is a one-time sawmill town whose railside buildings and main street have virtually vanished. Here are overgrown yards, foundations and the sole main-street survivor, an old hotel.

It began around 1895 when Father A. Desaulniers lead a group of French Canadian settlers into newly opened farmlands north of Lake Nipissing. Known initially as St. Anne de Desaulniers, the settlement claimed little more than a store and post office, while the farmers spent much of their time in logging camps. With the arrival of the Canadian Northern Railway in 1905, a sawmill was built beside the station, which was originally given the name Poincaré.

As the town prospered, hotels and stores lined the main street which led to the station, and the cross street which ran parallel to the tracks. A station agent's house and homes for section crews crowded close to the station. Beside the tracks stood the sawmill and the water tower. A new church was opened in 1916 to replace Father Desaulniers' original place of worship.

As roads were paved and improved, villagers took their shopping needs to the larger village of Field, just 7 km (4 miles) away, or to Sturgeon Falls, a much larger town located on Highway 17, the Trans Canada Highway.

When the CNR converted from steam to diesel, automatic signalling replaced station agents, passenger service was discontinued, and rail operations at Desaulniers ended. The station and water tower were removed, as were the various other railway buildings. Today even the tracks are gone. As the timber supply became depleted, and as farming proved uneconomical, the rural population declined dramatically.

While a scattering of homes survive on the highway, the former main street is silent now, the station and mill long vanished. Although the two homes are still occupied, the lone hotel stands silent. A solitary railway cabin weathered the wind and snow until it finally collapsed into a pile of rubble.

Although nothing remains of the station, the foundation of the water tower protrudes prominently from the weeds by the former private crossing. Of the other buildings that once made Desaulniers a hopeful settlement, only overgrown yards remain.

Desaulniers lies on Highway 539, 7 km (4 miles) west of Highway 64, north of Sturgeon Falls.

FRENCH RIVER

Prior to the arrival of the railways in northeastern Ontario, the shores of northern Georgian Bay contained more than two dozen sawmills, each of which could boast its own townsite. The confusing maze of rocky channels that constitutes the mouth of the mighty French River saw the rise of the large, but short-lived, mill town of "French River." Despite rocky terrain that hampered construction and its remoteness from markets, the site on the main channel of the French River was the gateway to a vast and rich stand of timber.

In the late 1870s the Walkerton Lumber Company began operating a small sawmill. Sam Wabb, who operated a small trading post, laid out a townsite of eight houses for the mill workers. The little community became known as Wabbtown. The next year Thomas Bolger laid out a larger company townsite and named it Copananing.

Following the establishment of the Ontario Lumber Company mills in 1889, a thriving town of 250 burst into existence. In addition to the two sawmills, there were three hotels including the Queen's Hotel, the Copananing Hotel and Joe Kelly's, two stores, operated by S.E. Wabb and Company and J.W. Jeffrey respectively, two churches, Presbyterian and Roman Catholic, and S.H. Davis' fishing company. Several crude frame homes lined the short dirt road, which only ventured a very short distance inland from the wharf. A small jail was also added to the landscape, although the history of its occupants remains unrecorded.

In their heyday the mills presented an awesome spectacle, as J.C. Hamilton discovered on one trip in the 1890s: "Next day we visited French River ... a great lumber centre with two mills, immense piles of pine boards and long elevated tramways for the removing and hauling of lumber." So massive were the log booms surrounding the mills that the regular steamers were often prevented from making their scheduled stop.

About this time Georgian Bay was becoming popular as a summer recreation ground. Tourists, lured by the romance and beauty of the bay's islands and waters, began to frequent lumber company hotels. An 1892 advertisement in the *Parry Sound Colonial* promoted the Queen's Hotel: "Tourists will find this is a first-class house. Good fishing and shooting in close proximity. The wines, liquors and cigars are the best. Billiard Room and Barber shop in connection."

Bare, rocky terrain and isolation prohibited any settlement that was unrelated to the milling operation. Thus, a decade or so later, when the mills closed and the mill workers left, the village of French River died. Most of its buildings were moved to new locations, many to a new mill location at Pickerel Landing Village.

Because of its isolation and local restrictions on new buildings, the mouth of the French River has largely escaped the cottage boom. Aside from a few fishing camps and marinas scattered among the rocky islands, the area has remained relatively unaltered over the decades since the closure of the mills. At the site of the one-time village there remain the sunken boilers of lumber company tugs and a few stone walls and foundations, overgrown by bushes and weeds, and occupied now only by rattlesnakes. The site is not accessible by road and is a lengthy boat ride from the nearest marina at Key River.

The main street of the mill town of French River was laid out along impossibly rocky terrain.

Today, shrubs (and rattlesnakes) have overtaken the site of French River village.

GARGANTUA

Created in 1944, Lake Superior Provincial Park contains some of Canada's most stunningly beautiful wilderness scenery, vistas of mountain and lake that attracted landscape painter such as members of Canada's Group of Seven. From the 1870s to the 1940s those rocky coves also sheltered half a dozen fishing colonies that huddled in the coves that indented the area's remote shores and islands.

Most were indentured to commercial fishing companies, which outfitted the fishermen, sent tugs to purchase the catch and often ran the steamships that linked the remote communities. One of those companies, the Dominion Transportation Company, provided the vital link between the offshore fishing villages on Michipicoten Island and the Lizard Islands, and Gargantua located on the mainland.

Named by the *voyageurs* after the fictional giant in Rabelais' *Gargantua and Pantagruel*, Gargantua was typical of most remote fishing settlements. Hidden behind a headland and safe from Superior's fury, an icehouse, net shed, warehouse and a few homes hugged the shore. In later years tourist cabins and squatters' shanties appeared as well. Small steamers like the *Caribou* and the *Manitou* called regularly, battling waves and the ever-present fog. When caught in the fog, captains could listen to the sound of their whistles echoing off the rocky shoreline to guide their vessels into the safety of the harbour.

By the late 1940s those whistles had been silenced, the two ships having been taken out of service in 1939 and 1942 respectively. A few years later, the great lakes fishery itself collapsed, a victim of over-fishing and the invasion of the predatory sea lamprey. The era of the summer fishing villages was over, and Gargantua became a ghost town. In 1968 it was incorporated into Lake Superior Provincial Park and is a popular destination for hikers using the park's shoreline trail, or campers on the wide sandy beach.

The remains of the village include the site of two wharves, a couple of collapsing structures and a row of foundations along the overgrown shore of the west side of the harbour. The site of the tourist cabins, which stood along the beach at the north end, is now a small campground. Out in the harbour the boiler of the vessel *Columbus*, which caught fire and had to be set loose from the wharf, peers above the water.

Gargantua Road leads west from Highway 17 near the south boundary of Lake Superior Provincial Park, which is located between Wawa and Sault Ste. Marie. At the start of the road, an information kiosk allows users to deposit their day use fees. From this point a winding dirt road leads for 14 km (9 miles) to a small parking lot where a trail sign announces "Gargantua Harbour, 2 km." A flat obstacle-free path leads to the site, about a 20-minute walk away.

During its heyday, the harbour at Gargantua was a busy spot.

A former fishing cabin recalls
busier times in the peaceful
harbour at Gargantua.

The Laurentian mill was one of several that operated at the town of Gold Rock.

Mine buildings still lurk in the woods where Gold Rock briefly flourished.

GOLD ROCK

In 1898 gold fever swept North America as cries of "gold" echoed from the distant Yukon gold fields. But by 1900, disheartened gold-seekers had begun seeking other gold fields. Many turned their attention to northwestern Ontario and the Manitou Lakes in particular.

While dozens of diggings and discoveries dotted the shores of the Manitou Lakes, the most spectacular finds were those in Trafalgar Bay, a swampy inlet in the northeast corner of Upper Manitou Lake. On these shores optimistic mine companies built more than a dozen mines, and the miners added their own boisterous little town, Gold Rock.

W.A. Blackstone's Bigmaster Mine led Gold Rock into life. By November, 1901, Blackstone had completed a shafthouse, a stamp mill and a sawmill that cut 10,000 board feet of lumber per day. Blackstone lured miners with "high western salaries," as one mining inspector referred to them, and by reducing shifts to eight hours. The Bigmaster's mining community boasted a manager's house, a boarding house, a cookery and several log cabins, as well as the mill and mine buildings. But by the fall of 1902 the deposit had yielded a meagre $5,000 worth of gold.

Most of Gold Rock's mines were similarly small and short-lived. The Little Master, located on an extension of the Bigmaster vein, shafted in 1903 and then closed temporarily in 1904 and 1905. In 1906, after another burst of activity, the power house burned and the Little Master closed for good.

The largest of the Gold Rock mines began when Anthony Blum opened the Laurentian mine, moving his operations from the less profitable Detola mine. The mining camp that developed around Laurentian included a laboratory, a telephone connection to the CPR station at Wabigoon and electricity for the workers' houses.

The heart of the mining activity was the village of Gold Rock, which grew up at the Manitou Lake landing on a townsite with 63 lots on four streets. Gold Rock boomed from a small village of tents and log houses in 1897 to a prosperous community featuring a store, a hotel, a school, an oil storage shed, stables and several private dwellings, as well as, it is said, entertainment for gentlemen.

Rocky wagon roads wound from the village through the woods to the scattered mining camps. Frame and log cabins dotted the roadsides, while the boarding houses and managers' homes clustered around the head-frames. It was a loosely knit community that numbered 500 at its peak.

Gold Rock's link with the outside world was a tortuous 11 km (6.8 mile) logging road that lurched through swamps and over outcrops northeasterly to Lake Minnehaha, where steamers shuttled miners and supplies to the boom town of Wabigoon on the CPR.

The big blow came when the Laurentian mine ran dry. Its operators had been secretly high-grading the reserves and, with the best ore gone, they walked away. Its closing heralded Gold Rock's demise. Intermittent activity continued even through the 1940s, but the community was dead.

Surprisingly, a small number of Gold Rock's buildings have survived the decades, although time and new cottages have increasingly altered the site. The old hotel, the store and a few dwellings were demolished for a fishing camp. The school remained intact until 1972, its books still in place on the desks. Sadly, local vandals removed the books, the desks and finally the building itself.

Still, a few remains yet lurk in the woods. Two kilometres from the townsite, beside the old wagon road, a small miners' cemetery lies hidden in the woods. The Laurentian, Detola and Bigmaster mines all retain skeletons of their mills, and a few of the original buildings and log cabins, although most are now collapsing shells.

Access to the site is difficult. While a trail leads through the woods from Highway 502 south of Dryden, a number of fly-in fishing camps lie along the Manitou Lakes and provide water access to the long-lost town of Gold Rock.

GOUDREAU

oudreau began in 1912 as a station and watering stop on the Algoma Central Railway. Then, with the discovery of gold and the opening of the Cline mine, Goudreau boomed as a jumping off point for the gold fields. At its peak, Goudreau could boast 200 residents. After a lull in mining, new mines began to open, including the Emily, the Algold and the Edward. The ACR built a two-storey station, while a hotel, a bank, two stores, a boarding house, a school, and private homes appeared on Goudreau's twisting streets. For a time a theatre operated in a private home.

Because the configuration of rock and lake prevented the village from having a geometric street pattern, most of the residents lived on twisting trails near the station. During the Second World War, most of Ontario's smaller gold mines shut down, their operations no longer protected as a wartime industry. Goudreau, however, survived the setback, and many townsfolk remained to work on the railway or in logging.

Although a few families still live in the area, and renewed mining activity has returned, much of Goudreau has been abandoned. While the store remains privately owned, its gas pump sits rusting. Sadly, the grand two-storey station was removed, leaving only foundations by the track, while other foundations, silent cabins and vestiges of mines stand beside the road.

The gold rush of the 1980s restored life to the Goudreau area where a pair of new mines had opened nearby. However, the Goudreau of yesterday will likely remain a ghost.

To reach Goudreau, follow Highway 519 from the Trans Canada about 45 km (28 miles) north of Wawa, 35 km (22 miles) to Dubreauville. From this modern and prosperous sawmill town, a dry-weather logging road leads for 25 km (15 miles) to Goudreau. A topographic map and local directions will prove useful.

Few of Goudreau's trackside cabins are left from the heady days of gold mining in the area.

While the former Goudreau store
has become a seasonal residence, the
gas pump has long been abandoned.

JACKFISH

Among all of Ontario's ghost towns, Jackfish enjoys one of the most scenic locations, and it is just 4 km (2.5 miles) from the busy Trans Canada Highway. It flourished for more than six decades.

In the 1870s a small group of Scandinavians established a fishing operation in the abundant waters of Jackfish Bay, a deep protected harbour on the north shore of Lake Superior. In 1884, as the CPR was building its transcontinental line along Superior's north shore, the railway laid out a construction townsite with a hotel, a dock, cabins and a trio of dynamite factories to blast the shore's ancient hard rocks. The deep sheltered harbour was the idea location for an 180 metre (600-foot) trestle coal dock to supply the railway's divisional towns of Cartier and Chapleau. The town quickly boomed, with both the railway and the fishing operations providing work for all who wanted it. At peak periods, up to 300 men worked the coal facilities.

Crammed with restless railway workers, Jackfish was often rowdy and lawless. The situation was so grim in 1885 that the *Port Arthur Weekly Herald* ran a feature on the thriving trades in whisky and gambling and the shadowy figures who ran them.

One such underworld figure was Ed McMartin. In November of that year, McMartin suddenly appeared in James McKay's boarding house looking for a man named Merrit, who was trying to move in on McMartin's exclusive bootlegging and gambling schemes. While McKay was trying to throw McMartin out, a brawl erupted and amidst the fisticuffs McMartin bit off McKay's finger. While McKay writhed in pain, MacMartin fled and hopped on board a departing freight train. Because he didn't want to stray too far from his illegal operations in Jackfish, however, he went no further than Cartier, where the railway police arrested him. While struggling to get free, he was shot and killed.

The rocky cliff-bound shore was a difficult location for a town, and the cabins, church, school, and boarding houses vied for the limited level space. When tourism and fishing derbies became more popular along Lake Superior's north shore, Jackfish added the Lakeview Hotel. As the social hub of the community, the Lakeview hosted dances and dinners, and was a haven for thirsty crews from visiting ships. Once the sound of the ship's whistle pierced the night air, tipsy sailors had to pick their way along darkened bouldery walkways to the dock. Brawls often erupted between rival bootleggers anxious to capture the local hotel business.

Scattered over the hillsides were a general store, two churches, a school and 30 houses. By the tracks stood the station, water tower and half a dozen CPR railway houses. The popularity of paintings by Ontario's Group of Seven artists attracted tourists to Jackfish. They arrived by rail to stay at the Lakeview Hotel. For many years Jackfish hosted a popular annual fishing derby, and was featured on postcards.

By the late 1940s, the era of the steam engine was fast fading. With the conversion of its engines to diesel, the CPR closed and dismantled its coal dock. A few years later, as a result of overfishing and the predations of the sea lamprey eel, the fisheries fell into decline. By the mid-1960s, Jackfish was a ghost town, and, despite visits by cottagers, it remains a ghost town.

Its ruins lie hidden by the bush and stretch for 500 metres (550 yards) along the shore. They include the foundations of the Roman Catholic church as well as those of the former water tower and the Lakeview Hotel.

Access to Jackfish is gained from the end of a garbage dump road just 4 km (2.5 miles) west of the Trans Canada Highway bridge that crosses the Steel River. From this point a narrow trail leads up a rocky ridge to Jackfish. A shorter 2 km (1.2 mile) route leads along the railway track, but because of the frequency of trains, it is not recommended.

After the harbour's half-century of existence, Jackfish's cabins have fallen totally vacant.

As this abandoned car testifies, it is no longer possible to drive into Jackfish.

KIOSK/FOSSMILL

By 1924 the pine in the limits of Quebec's Fasset Lumber Company were gone, and president S.J. Staniforth sent John McGibbon to appraise possible new timber stands in and around Algonquin Park in Ontario.

At a siding called Fossmill on the edge of Algonquin Park, Staniforth established a mill and a town. Along the track he built 35 homes, some one-and-a-half storeys high and large enough to accommodate three families. Soon afterward he built a wooden schoolhouse where, during Fossmill's boom years, 53 pupils fidgeted through the eight primary grades.

Two disastrous fires in three years wrote the end of the town's story. In 1932 smoke was spotted in the lumber-yard. As workers ran with fire hoses, the dry piles exploded into flames. Worker and supervisor toiled together, keeping the bucking hoses trained on the fire and bringing in pumps and water to prevent the conflagration from consuming the mill. In 1932 they succeeded, but in 1934 they were not so fortunate. One of Ontario's greatest lumber mills burned to the ground that year.

Upon learning that the large limits of the J.R. Booth Company only 18 kilometres (11 miles) to the east were available, Staniforth obtained permission from the province to erect a mill and town within the limits of Algonquin Park. A year later he moved to this new site, Kiosk, and Fossmill died. By 1940 the 35 houses in Fossmill had dwindled to 16 and by 1955 to six. Today, not one building stands and the road has become impassable to everything but all-terrain vehicles.

Before Staniforth arrived at the new site, the settlement on the shore of Kioshkakwi Lake contained only a handful of CNR section buildings and a small Booth lumber camp with a store, a bunkhouse and a cookery. These, however, would soon be swallowed up by Algonquin Park's largest town. On the shore of the lake beside the old Booth camp at the mouth of the Ausable River, Staniforth built his mill. For the first few years the population of 75 lived in the Booth bunkhouse or in one of a handful of cabins along the track. In 1938 he acquired a post office and named it Kiosk, the shortened name of the lake.

Staniforth carefully planned his new empire. In 1943, on the east side of the river overlooking his mill, he built the first of two townsites. On the west bank of the river he added a second townsite. As the population swelled to 250, the town acquired a Roman Catholic church, a new four-room school and piped water. Electricity came from a small power plant on the river.

After work and on weekends, the townsfolk would gather at the baseball diamond, skating rink or recreation hall in the former school. Although never an incorporated municipality, Kiosk was governed by a small elected council that supervised electricity, water supply and snow ploughing.

Kiosk kept growing, and by 1961 its 350 residents lived in 75 houses. Despite the arrival of a paved highway, the town never realized the full range of stores and services that a place of its size would normally expect. As was typical of a company town, no store was allowed to compete with the single company store. And liquor, at least technically, was prohibited.

The Staniforth mill at Kiosk
before it burned in the 1970s
and was relocated.

Where 70 houses, along with a
church and school, once lined
Kiosk's roads, the forest has
now taken over.

Before being terminated by
the Ontario government,
Kiosk contained 70 houses,
many like these.

In 1969 Staniforth's lease expired and his troubles began. Having determined that a residential community is not a use appropriate for a provincial park, the Ontario Department of Lands and Forests refused to renew the mill lease for more than one year at a time. Four years later, when the huge mill burned to the ground, the government denied Staniforth permission to rebuild. As the timber limits were still good, he rebuilt just outside the park boundary, and residents easily commuted the short distance. Although they owned their Kiosk homes, they did not own the land, and the department, by then known as the Ministry of Natural Resources, wanted it back. Their park "master plan" designated the area as "wilderness" and homes did not belong.

But Kiosk refused to fall without a fight. Recruiting federal and provincial politicians, residents pleaded for their homes and offered to exchange a private wilderness area adjacent to the park for their town. The ministry stood firm.

The townsfolk did, however, win a small victory: those who wished could remain until they chose to sell, at which time they had to offer their homes to the ministry. Today, no original building remains. A canoe launching facility and ministry permit office now occupy the site of the old station and Booth bunkhouse, while a campground sprawls on the site of the mill. On both sides of the river, dirt lanes and paths in the young forest follow the village's one-time streets, and a few foundations can still be found in the underbrush.

A guidebook entitled *Experience Route 630* lists the historic and natural attractions that line the route from Highway 17 to the ghost town. Kiosk is about 60 km (37 miles) east of North Bay.

Kiosk was not Algonquin Park's only ghost town. Others that can still be traced along the CN line, now lifted, include small section hamlets like Daventry, which still contains its former schoolhouse, and Achray, which is another launch site for park canoists. Brent was a major divisional town on this line, with stores, houses and a bunkhouse for the train crews. All have been removed except a few cottages. J.R. Booth's railway also gave rise to a string of mill towns, the largest of which was Mowat on Canoe Lake. It later became a popular tourist destination with a pair of hotels. One guest was renowned painter Tom Thomson, whose untimely death is still an unsolved mystery. A few early houses remained as cottages, with three graves and the remains of the last of the Gilmour Lumber Company's mills nearby. Other sawmill settlements like Rain Lake, Brule Lake and Rock Lake have vanished with little trace.

An early boarding house survives on Lochalsh's grid network of streets.

The first railway station at Lochalsh was a simple wooden structure built by the CPR. *(CP Archives)*

LOCHALSH

A s Canada's railway companies projected their steel rails out through the northern Ontario bushland, small communities grew at trackside. Most were small villages to house section crews and station agents. Others grew around sawmills built to tap the previously inaccessible timber stands. A few boomed, as prospectors leapt off the trains to answer the tempting call of "gold."

Located midway between the CPR divisional towns of White River and Chapleau, Lochalsh began as one of those section villages. When gold fever infected the area in the 1920s, Lochalsh added a school, three stores and two hotels (the Prospect and the Royal George), as well as a boarding house, while simple cabins were hurriedly constructed on the small grid network of streets. At its height, Lochalsh housed 200 residents.

The centre of town was Hang Fong's restaurant, where thirsty prospectors and railway crews could enjoy their fill of contraband liquor. To confuse the police on their regular raids, Fong built a moveable staircase, which allowed the patrons upstairs time enough to hide the evidence while the police searched for the evasive stairs.

Lochalsh was connected by a crude road with its sister village of Goudreau on the Algoma Central Railway about 25 km (15 miles) to the west. Between them stood the Cline Mine with a village of its own, consisting of about two dozen houses. A taxi operated by Alma Lavoie bounced over the narrow potholed trails, shuttling residents between all three centres.

While the mine prospered, so, too, did the trio of villages. During the Second World War, many of Ontario's northern mines closed down to allow their workers to enlist. After the conflict ended, many mines did not re-open. In 1946 the townsite at the Cline Mine was dismantled, and Goudreau and Lochalsh became ghost towns. The school remained open until 1962, while the post office continued to handle mail until 1967.

The grid network of Lochalsh's streets can still be followed. Along it lie several old railway-era buildings, including a one-time tenement house, the large green Lavoie house, which in later years housed both the school and two churches, and, in a former store, a year-round hunting and fishing lodge with the descriptive name of "Open Season Sometimes Sno'd Inn." Throughout the remaining townsite, bush hides the tumble-down ruins of the cabins and houses that Lochalsh's residents once called home.

Lochalsh is accessible via logging roads from the busy mill town of Dubreuilville, which is north of Wawa. The Magpie Industrial Road leads 3 km (1.8 miles) to a T intersection. From here the route runs left for another 1 km (0.6 miles), forking right and crossing the railway tracks. Another right turn takes the route 14 km (8.5 miles) to a fork in the road. The left fork leads another 10 km (6 miles) to signs that point to the tourist camps and Lochalsh. A more comfortable mode of transportation, however, is VIA Rail's service from White River.

Cribbings in Michael's Bay hark back to
its early days as a mill town and port of
entry into Manitoulin Island.

MICHAEL'S BAY

Although Manitoulin Island contains many old villages whose glory days are behind them, Michael's Bay is described as Manitoulin's "only official ghost town." Situated off Lake Huron's north shore, Manitoulin Island lay in the path of the great 1860s and 1870s lumbering boom. Toronto entrepreneur Robert Lyon saw it coming and in 1868 built a sawmill on the Manitou River on the island's southeast shore. Rapids powered the mill, while the sandy riverbank was ideal for workers' homes.

"Stumptown," as Michael's Bay was first called, became Manitoulin's first permanent white settlement and the port of entry for its homesteaders. In 1888 a townsite plan renamed the village Michael's Bay and showed 18 blocks and 250 lots. Queen Street led to the dock a short distance away, while King Street wound through the bush to an upstart fishing station named South Baymouth 8 km (5 miles) away. However, the plan was largely ignored; houses simply straddled lots or stood in the middle of roads.

Michael's Bay swelled to 20 houses, a store, a blacksmith, a school and two hotels. One, the Bayview House, became a popular destination for American tourists. While the mill and bushworkers pushed Michael's Bay's seasonal population to 400, the permanent population numbered around 100. In 1906 the *Union Farmers' Directory* reported that C.L. Wedgerfield ran the general store where Miss E. Wedgerfield made dresses. Robert Gault operated the post office, P.L. Clark worked the blacksmith shop and James Hilson made wagons. The school also served as a community centre and church. For a time the town was home to a colony of fishermen; however, the protected harbour at South Baymouth eventually lured them from the more exposed shores of Michael's Bay.

The centre of the town's activity remained Lyon's saw- and shingle mill. Boards, lath, shingles, rails, posts and ties were piled onto trains and dragged over wooden rails to tugs and schooners waiting at the docks.

Although Lyon had paid only $2,000 for 60 square km (40 square miles) of timber, he felt unencumbered by his boundaries and was accused of taking lumber from Crown Land. Furthermore, his personal bills put his Michael's Bay Trading Company seriously in debt. Then, in 1890, when his wood mansion mysteriously burned, he sold out and fled to Toronto to lead the less hazardous life of a member of the provincial legislature.

By 1910 pioneer settlers had moved in and begun burning the slash left by the lumberjacks. One such fire, unattended and whipped by sudden winds, raced toward Michael's Bay. Helpless to stop it, the townspeople fled with what they could carry. When the flames finally died, most of the cabins were smouldering ash. Disheartened, most turned their backs on the town and moved inland. However, Mitchell's boarding house, the school and the mill-manager's house survived until 1927, when the mill finally closed, its long-dwindling timber supply exhausted. By then the village population was a mere twelve.

The intervening years have claimed almost everything that was Michael's Bay. Now, all that remain are depressions in the ground, the mill foundations and the cribbing from the King Street Bridge. The newly formed Michael's Bay Historical Society has taken on the mission of buying the townsite and restoring the mill, store, blacksmith shop and lighthouse.

The site lies at the end of Michael's Bay Road, halfway between Providence Bay and South Baymouth.

Chimneys are all that survive of
what was once a Milnet building.

MILNET

ilnet began as "Sellwood Junction," a remote station and watering stop for the Canadian Northern Railway. A siding led from this point to the large townsite and mine at Sellwood, a short distance to the west. When the Moose Mountain iron ore mine at Sellwood first swung into operation in 1907, it was isolated. The following year, the Canadian Northern Railway laid its tracks to the new mining town, and Sellwood briefly became the railway's northern terminus. Then, when the railway continued laying its tracks northward to Foleyet and beyond, it did so from Sellwood Junction, and the mine was relegated to a spur line location.

Because nearby Onaping Lake offered an opportunity to boom logs from a vast region, lumbering began in earnest shortly after the line was extended. In 1917 the Marshay Lumber Company built a saw- and planing mill at the junction, and laid out the large townsite that is evident today. That same year its name was changed to Milnet.

In its 22 years, Marshay cut more than 100 million board feet of white, red and jack pine in their busy Milnet mill, while on the linear streets beside the track they added several dozen two-storey company houses as well as a boarding house. Water was provided from a pump located by the boarding house. Residents, who numbered about 200, received regular visits from a doctor and a priest, as the community lacked a church building.

Disaster came to Milnet twice – the sawmill burned in 1933 and the planing mill a year later. By 1940 most residents had left and the post office closed down in 1944. Because the residents could not re-sell their homes, these buildings were destroyed when left vacant.

Of those grand homes, only three survive today, and are used now only seasonally. Foundations and stone chimneys mark the remaining sites. The rest of the townsite has become a vast overgrown meadow of debris and rubble.

Meanwhile, in the bush by the lake, the shell of the old mill waits to be rediscovered.

The Sellwood townsite was much larger than the site at Milnet. The mining town, with its population at a peak of 1,500, contained a 100-room boarding and nearly a dozen businesses. When the mine closed in 1920, Sellwood became a ghost town. However, when a pelletizing plant opened in 1964, the remaining buildings were removed, leaving only a few foundations and a cemetery.

Milnet lies 12 km (7.5 miles) north of Capreol near the end of Regional Road 84.

The shell of the Milnet mill can still be found in the woods.

NESTERVILLE

Straddling Highway 17, west of the scenic community of Thessalon, sits the partial ghost town of Nesterville. Another of the North Shore's many sawmill towns, Nesterville began in 1907, when Frank Nester and H. Bishop of the Thessalon Lumber Company bought land on Lake Huron's MacBeth Bay and built a sawmill. The mill buzzed night and day for more than two decades until the pine stands were depleted.

In its heyday, the town consisted of a church, a school, stores, a post office and a population that peaked at 400. A small CPR railway station also served the community and carried passengers to the larger towns of Sault Ste. Marie to the west and Blind River to the east. The mill closed in the 1930s and never reopened. Residents moved away, many to the mills in nearby Thessalon. By the 1950s, the population had dropped to little more than 100, and in 1960 the post office finally closed.

McFadden Road served as the village's main street. The station stood a short distance to the east where McFadden Road intersected with Nesterville Road. When the Trans Canada Highway was widened and straightened in the 1970s, it cut a swath along the south side of McFadden Road, removing many of the buildings in that location. Others survive on the north side of the road beside the village's former main street. These include a handful of original homes, some abandoned, along with a pair of more recent houses. Overgrown lots indicate the sites of the store and what was a string of cabins.

Nesterville lies on Highway 17 west of Nesterville Road, 6 km (3.7 miles) west of Thessalon.

One of Nesterville's many workers' cabins is ready to succumb to old age.

This house is one of Nesterville's
few more substantial homes.

Few of Nicholson's abandoned cabins
have survived the effects of weather.

NICHOLSON

Tall grasses and young trees are now growing up around the collapsed shell of Nicholson's Roman Catholic church; its old cabins are now mere piles of lumber. Yet, until recently, Nicholson had been one of Ontario's most complete and more photogenic ghost towns.

It was around 1900 that James Austin and George Nicholson walked away from their jobs as store manager and railway engineer respectively. Recognizing the pressing demand for railway ties for the CPR's expanding network of rail lines, they built a tie mill on the shore of Windermere Lake, from which they could access a vast hinterland of pine.

The early years at Nicholson were quiet, with only a small mill, a bunkhouse, a cookery and a manager's house making up the settlement. A converted boxcar served as the "station." In 1910 Austin and Nicholson enlarged their limits, expanded the mill and added to the town a school, a company store, a boarding house and two dozen workers' cabins. The bunkhouse stood two storeys high and contained 68 beds and, it is said, an ample supply of spittoons.

These were the town's boom years. Facing the railway siding that curved into the crescent-shaped peninsula were the company store, the school, Scheffield's boarding house, a row of cabins and the town's social centre, Pottney's pool room. Across the tracks from the station was the Anglican church, while on a hill behind the track stood the grand homes of Austin and Nicholson. Later the partners added a theatre and behind their executive homes a tennis court. The residents could also enjoy such amenities as a post office, free grocery delivery, electricity and police protection.

Most Saturday nights Nicholson came alive with square dancing in the school, but the folks at Nicholson especially looked forward to the arrival of Omer Lauzon. Every few weeks, Lauzon would climb down from the train with his large movie projector and a stack of Hollywood's latest silent movies. A sheaf of music was ready for any local who would brave the keyboards of a piano to accompany the movie

When a new two-storey school replaced the original building, the first school was re-incarnated as the town's Catholic church, necessary for the town's primarily French population. Indeed so small was the Protestant congregation that the local Anglican bishop expressed surprise at its very existence. "You imply the existence of a church," he wrote to the town's student minister. "I would be obliged if you would kindly send me a brief description of it in order that it may be entered in our books."

By 1924 the mill was turning out two and a half million railway ties a year, enough for 2500 km (1,550 miles) of track. In that year, a two-storey school replaced the earlier building and the CPR added a larger station with agents' quarters in the second floor.

Nicholson's days ended when the mill burned in 1933 and the company shifted operations to its other mills. From 800, the population plummeted to twenty-five. One by one, the store, school, churches and station closed.

By the 1970s Nicholson had become a classic ghost town, with its cabins forlorn and weathered and a main street of large false-fronted buildings. Indeed, historians from the Ministry of Natural Resources, then responsible for both heritage and crown lands, recommended that Nicholson become Ontario's first ghost town park. The ministry ignored the report, however, and shortly afterward the main street burned.

Although a few of the original homes are now used as summer cottages, most of the old village has deteriorated badly. Foresight by a provincial government department three decades ago might have left Ontarians with a unique ghost town legacy. Now, as wind and snow have taken their toll, it is too late.

Nicholson can be reached by train from Chapleau or by boat from Shoals Provincial Park on Windermere Lake.

PAKESLEY/LOST CHANNEL

Well before Ontario's railway lines had penetrated the forests of northern Parry Sound, lumber companies were using the province's many rivers to raft logs to their mills. Beginning in 1890, the Victoria Harbour Lumber Company floated its logs down the Pickerel River to Georgian Bay and then boomed them across the bay to their mills at Victoria Harbour.

After the Canadian Pacific and the Canadian Northern Railways extended their lines into the area, the lumber companies could build their mills close to the tracks and ship out sawn lumber by train much more cheaply. Shortly after the Canadian Northern Railway reached the area in 1905, the Lauder, Spears and Howland Company assumed the limits of the Victoria Harbour Lumber Company, and, on the Pickerel River at the head of a deep bay known as Lost Channel, they built a new mill. From

the mill, teams of horses strained to haul the lumber to the railway siding of Mowat over 20 km (12.5 miles) of bush road that was beset by mud, rocks and fallen trees.

In 1912 the CPR completed its Bolton to Sudbury subdivision, a route that lay much closer to the mill. Another set of new owners, the Schroeder Mills and Timber Company, replaced the impassable road with a railway spur line to the CPR called the Key Valley Railway.

Nearby the mill at Lost Channel, a village appeared; it included a bunkhouse, a cookery, a hospital, a school, a blacksmith and more than a dozen single cabins for workers with families. At Pakesley, the junction of the Key Valley Railway with the CPR, there stood a hotel, a post office, a store, a restaurant and an Ontario Department of Lands and Forests fire headquarters. By the track, the CPR added their station, a wooden two-storey Tuscan red building that

The Key Valley Railway connected the mills at Lost Channel with the busy railway junction of Pakesley.

contained seven second-floor rooms for the agent and his family. Several cabins and barns clustered by the tracks as well.

The first of the two townsites to become a ghost town was Lost Channel. By 1933 the timber limits were exhausted, and the mill closed down. When the workers left, the forest began to reclaim the village.

Pakesley, however, went on to survive another 25 years. The Department of Lands and Forests continued to staff its fire tower until the late 1950s, when most such towers were replaced with aircraft surveillance. During this period the hotel and store closed as well. Then, in the early 1970s, the last of Pakesley's functions ended when the CPR demolished the station, along with most of the stations along its Sudbury branch.

Pakesley lies at the CPR crossing on Highway 522

just 5 km (3 miles) east of Highway 69, about 80 km (50 miles) north of Parry Sound.

Here, on the east side of the track, and north of the highway, four former homes, used mainly as seasonal dwellings, line a village lane. South of the road, shrubs and young trees hide the remains of barns and homes. On the west side of the track are the sites of the station and the Lands and Forests buildings.

Lost Channel lies 15 km (9 miles) further east on Highway 522 at the end of the road that leads to Lost Channel Lodge, the building that served as the mill town's boarding house. The waters of the cove beside the lodge contain the cribbings of the dock, while the young forest hides the rubble of the old village.

This abandoned cabin in Pakesley
lies behind a growth of bushes.

This early building in Pickerel Landing
is now surrounded by a trailer park.

PICKEREL LANDING VILLAGE

The sawmill town of Pickerel Landing, on the south shore of the Pickerel River, started up when the mill in the town of French River, which had been located on Georgian Bay, ended its own operations. In 1912 the Pine Lake Lumber Company acquired the limits of Ontario Lumber Company and moved those operations from French River to the shores of Pine Lake on the Pickerel River. Here they could be closer to the newly opened CPR line between Toronto and Sudbury. Following a devastating fire, the Trottier Lumber Company of Bigwood took over the mill and operated it until it closed in 1950.

Beside the mill a town developed which included a store, five houses and a Catholic church, all situated close to the landing. Further inland a network of streets accommodated a school, another boarding house and about a dozen homes, both single and duplex, along with a second store. East of the mill "Newton-town" was a neighbourhood of half a dozen homes belonging to the many members of the Newton family who had migrated from the original mill village at French River. By the railway track the CPR erected a two-storey station covered with wood shingle siding. Sheds and a watering tower stood nearby.

Despite the removal of the mill, the community did not die out completely. Tourists had started to discover the French River area when the CPR established its own resort known as the French River Bungalow Camp. Guests at this remote location included such Hollywood legends as Marilyn Monroe.

The Canadian Northern Railway added its own line across the French and Pickerel rivers, and more resorts and cottages sprang up. In the 1960s the Trans Canada Highway confirmed the age of automobile travel for vacationers, and today the shores of the French and Pickerel rivers are lined with summer homes and seasonal cottages. Among these, at the site of Pickerel Landing Village, is a trailer park that opened on the grounds of the mill.

The early village buildings that are still present amid the RVs and campers include an original house by the dock, and another old home and the former boarding house, which stand further south. Part of the grid street pattern can still be seen as well.

The Ontario government has opened a large interpretive facility near Highway 69. The centre, which overlooks the French River, hosts displays recounting the natural and human history of the historic river.

Pickerel Landing Village lies east of Highway 69 at the end of the Pickerel Landing Road.

Few of these Pickerel Landing buildings survived the tourist boom.

SILVER CENTRE

The scenic Lorrain Valley stretches south from North Cobalt to the remote silver fields of Silver Centre. Following the silver rush of 1903 to the remote rocks of what would become the fabulous boom town of Cobalt, prospectors spread out through the dense forests to find evidence of more silver. In 1907 silver seekers Bob Jowsey, Charles Keeley and James Woods found their bonanza. It lay some 30 km (18 miles) south of Cobalt near the shores of Lake Temiskaming.

Soon several mines were being opened. Although most were duds, or short-lived, a few managed to produce enough silver to require a town. These were the Keeley Mine, the Wettlaufer Mine and later the Frontier Mine.

The boom town of Silver Centre grew quickly around these later silver finds. Its population peaked at 700 during the 1920s; most of the residents lived in boarding houses near the mines or in simple cabins that lined the twisting roads between mines. Managers, however, could enjoy larger homes further from the noise of the mining operations.

Although little more than a tent and shack village, Silver Centre could claim a restaurant run by the Pickerings, and a store operated by the Provenchers. Bill Bulger offered the community's only outside link, with his daily summer steamer service on Lake Temiskaming. In 1924 a daily rail link was opened to Cobalt, and Silver Centre acquired a two-storey wooden station. On weekends the rail cars were filled with thirsty miners heading to the bars of North Cobalt and Haileybury, or to the illicit booze cans of Cobalt itself.

Despite its remoteness and the harshness of its living conditions, Silver Centre had a strength of character that belied its size. Indeed its robust hockey team was more than game to take on all comers.

But as with most mining towns, it did not last. By 1926 the Keeley and newer Frontier veins had run dry. The population fell by half, and train service was cut to three trips a week. In 1943 the last of the mines closed and Silver Centre quickly died. Isolated and completely dependent on silver, it could fall back on no other lifeline once the mines closed.

From North Cobalt, 6 km (3.5 miles) east of Cobalt on Highway 11B, Highway 567 winds for 30 km (18.5 miles) through the scenic pastoral Lorrain Valley. Less than 2 km (1.2 miles) past the last of the farmhouses, the road leaves the valley and struggles up a rocky ridge. Here a trail of cinders, wide enough for a car, forks right from the highway. It twists and lurches until it reaches a pair of large grey shells, the only remains of the mine operations.

An even rougher trail that branches to the left leads to the townsite a short distance further on, where only rusting artifacts, rubble and foundations remain from the booming town that once was Silver Centre.

Silver Centre once rivalled
Cobalt as a leading producer of
silver. These mining buildings
formed part of the community's
social centre.

Before it was restored, the Silver Islet store looked decidedly ghostly.

Most of the Silver Islet town-site lay on the mainland. This view is from the roof of the large general store.

SILVER ISLET

For millennia, Skull Islet sat dwarfed beneath the looming limestone plateau known as the Sleeping Giant, endlessly washed by Lake Superior's relentless waves. Beneath the tiny shoal lay the veins of what would be Canada's richest silver deposit. The Montreal Mining company acquired the site in 1845, but more than 20 years passed before Thomas MacFarlane was sent to assess the site. However, the difficulty posed by the waves impeded his efforts at extracting the little rock's wealthy treasure.

In 1868, the company was sold to Major Alexander Sibley of Detroit, who sent mining engineer William Frue to conquer the waves. Frue's first few breakwaters proved helpless against the lake's onslaught. Finally, with a more substantial barrier in place, Frue added the mine shafts and boarding houses and began to wrest the silver from the beneath the lake.

In 1873 a vicious spring storm sent waves hurtling over the breakwater and washed the buildings into the lake. Undaunted, Frue went back to work, adding four boarding houses, a library and a medical clinic to the island, while on the mainland a village began to take shape. Along the shore, and protected from the lake by Burnt Island, were the 40 cabins of the mine workers, the grand homes of the managers, a customs house, two churches, a bank and a five-cell jail. A 50-stamp mill was erected to process the silver laden ore using Frue's own invention known to this day as the Frue vanner. By the wharf a large three-storey store catered to the town's many needs.

Out on the shoal, however, the veins were starting to thin. By 1883 the mine had yielded silver worth more than $3 million, making it the richest silver vein ever mined in Canada to that date. As the shafts were dug ever deeper, coal-fired pumps were needed to keep out the water. But the lake froze over early that year, and the coal boat remained stuck fast on the south shore. The vital coal did not arrive. By March the existing supply had run out, and the pumps fell silent. Silver Islet's days were over.

After the miners left, the residents of nearby Port Arthur and Fort William began to enjoy summer excursions to the clear air of the little community. Eventually, the solidly built cabins became summer cottages, which they remain to this day.

Although a ghost town, Silver Islet has not been entirely abandoned. The string of sturdy miners' cabins that line the shore road are still well maintained. At the end of that road are the graves of the Silver Islet cemetery. In the summertime, cottagers sail and sunbathe, while the more hardy swim in Lake Superior's frigid waters. Many of the early buildings are gone, however, including the mill, the Catholic church and some of the grander homes. Newer homes now line several of the streets away from the lake. Happily, the town's most important building, the long-abandoned store, has been restored and is open once more for business. The permanent population of Silver Islet, however, remains at only eight.

The ghosts of Silver Islet lie at the end of Highway 587 south of the Trans Canada Highway east of Thunder Bay.

(A post-script: The individual primarily responsible for restoring the store, CBC announcer Lorne Saxeburg, died while on vacation in Malaysia in May of 2006.)

VICTORIA MINES

In 1889 Dr. Ludwig Mond and Dr. Karl Langer, two British metallurgists, discovered a way to perfectly separate nickel and copper. After being rebuffed by the Canada Copper Company (later to become INCO), Mond set out to put his process into practice. In 1899 he acquired a number of nickel prospects west of Sudbury, and opened the Mond Mine. South of the mine, he built a smelter close the CPR's Sault Ste. Marie line, and laid out the townsite of Victoria Mine.

Here, on a network of a half a dozen streets, were two schools (public and separate) a barber, a butcher, a bowling alley, four grocery stores and a pair of boarding houses. There were also an officials' clubhouse, a doctor's office, the company store and a jail. Except for Main Street, all streets were simply numbered. A wooden single-storey CPR train station offered service between the town and Sudbury. At its peak, Victoria Mines could claim over 500 residents (one of whom was hockey great, Hector "Toe" Blake of the Montreal Canadiens).

The mine itself was located 3 km (1.8 miles) to the north of the town, with a roasting yard between the two. Mond owned several prospects in the Sudbury and in 1913 opened a new smelter at Consiton closer to his other mines.

In addition, Consiton had better rail connections on the CPR's newly opened Toronto-to-Sudbury line, and was selected as a better site for the smelter.

Moving the smelter to Coniston meant the end of Victoria Mines. Company houses were sawed in half and moved to a different mine at Worthington a short distance to the west. Private homes were moved by their owners, many of them to Coniston, as were the two churches. Today only a solitary two-storey home lies in the town site, which is now split diagonally by Highway 737. A short distance east of the house, a trail leads north from the highway into what were once village streets lined with more than 50 buildings.

Today, the streets are paths in a meadow, and the site of the homes only discernible by the vague depressions beside them. A cement foundation is the only other evidence that any habitation might have been here at all.

At the Mond Mine, another townsite was laid out, one that lasted until 1923, but most of that area has been excavated for a gravel pit. Worthington too became a ghost town when its mine shafts caved in, taking much of the town with them.

A new smelting process perfected by Ludwig Mond led to the opening of the Mond mine and the establishment of the Victoria Mines townsite.

Victoria Mines last two homes (foreground and behind the trees) are now reduced to one.

Of the many houses and buildings that once stood in the Victoria Mines townsite, this is the last.

This painting shows the layout of the factory town of Patterson before the owners moved their operations to Woodstock in the 1870s.

CHAPTER 5

GOLDEN HORSESHOE
TRAILS

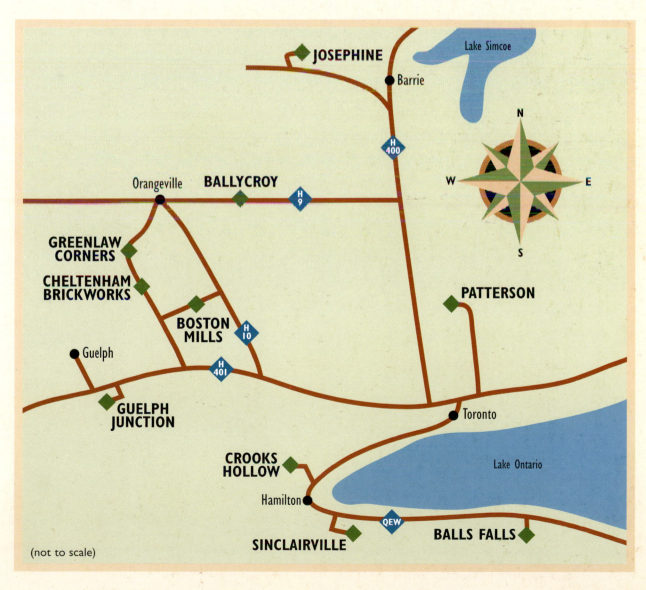

JOSEPHINE

Lake Simcoe

Barrie

H 400

N

W   E

S

Orangeville   BALLYCROY   H 9

PATTERSON

GREENLAW
CORNERS

CHELTENHAM
BRICKWORKS

BOSTON
MILLS   H 10

Guelph

H 401

Toronto

GUELPH
JUNCTION

Lake Ontario

CROOKS
HOLLOW

Hamilton

QEW

SINCLAIRVILLE   BALLS FALLS

(not to scale)

The ruins of the Balls Falls' woollen mill
lie beside the falls' upper cascade.

BALLS FALLS

What is today the ghost town of Balls Falls began in 1809 when the Ball brothers, John and George, built a wooden gristmill by a high thundering falls on Twenty Mile Creek in the heart of the Niagara Peninsula. Known as Glen Elgin, it had by the 1840s grown into one of the area's busiest industrial towns.

The gristmill and most of the town's houses lined the streets on a plateau above the lower waterfall, while the saw- and woollen mills stood in the canyon by the upper fall. Five storeys high, the woollen mill used eight looms to turn out jerseys of cashmere, tweed and flannel. An all-female staff lived in a boarding house beside the mill above the falls. The flourishing village also boasted a barrel maker, a blacksmith and two lime kilns, as well as a store and several houses.

On the flat between the two falls, Peter Mann Ball laid out an extensive townsite in anticipation of still greater growth. But the expansion never took place. During the 1850s, the Great Western Railway laid its rails well below the escarpment some distance north of Glen Elgin. The old village soon lost its importance as new industries located by the railway, and Glen Elgin gradually became a ghost town.

Thanks to the efforts of the Niagara Region Conservation Authority, the site is preserved. Of the old buildings, only the gristmill, a lime kiln and the Ball homestead have survived. Other historic buildings from the surrounding region, including a pioneer log cabin and a picturesque wooden church, have been relocated the Balls Falls park.

A trail from the parking lot follows the former village road along the west side of the river to the ruins of the woollen mill. Here the upper falls plunges over the rugged limestone lip of the Niagara Escarpment. On the hill behind the ruin, another path leads to the site of the boarding house, where only a rusting water pump survives to mark the location.

Interpretive plaques throughout the site recount the stories of the village and its various operations. The entrance to the conservation area lies a short distance south of the village of Vineland on Regional Road 24.

The mill at Balls Falls, which is now a museum, has been around since the place was called Glen Elgin.

BALLYCROY

Around 1820, on a creek that flowed through the Oak Ridge Moraine northwest of Toronto, Sam Beatty built Ballycroy's first sawmill. Later, a grist-mill, two stores and three hotels were added. The location represented the intersection of two of the region's most important routes, one that led to Toronto, the other to Orangeville. Dances in the hotels often lasted until dawn and the volatile mix of Orange and Catholic Irish frequently resulted in donnybrooks that spilled out onto the streets.

As one observer noted: "The ballroom (in Peter's Small's hotel) was notable for its splendour … enormous piles of eatables were laid out on the tables … dances lasted all night and far into the next day. It was usually decorous enough at first but was apt to degenerate rapidly as liquor circulated and not infrequently broke up in wild free-for-alls."

Then on the night of April 29, 1875, fire raced through the village and destroyed the blacksmith shop, the woodworking shop, three dwellings, a tavern and Peter Small's hotel. The real tragedy of the night that shocked the townsfolk was that three girls, who worked in the nearby millinery, were hopelessly trapped, and burned to death.

After the fire, Ballycroy never fully recovered. The railways had reached Palgrave just a short distance south, and businesses shifted to that town. The temperance movement killed business in the two remaining hotels, as it did throughout Ontario, while rural postal delivery eliminated the need for farmers to visit the general store for their mail. Then, with the arrival of the auto age, the old pioneer roads were rerouted to bypass Ballycroy, and

the town has since remained a backwater. As a result, the once-busy Orangeville Road has become an unused trail lined only with the cellar holes and foundations from the days when it served as the village's main street.

Fehely's Hotel managed to survive until 1985, when it was finally demolished. The McClelland Hotel and general store remain, and look little changed. The hotel portion still sports its porch and the boom-town façade marks the store.

Across the road, a weathered sign proclaiming "Ballycroy" marks the centre of the ghost village. Beside the sign, the old Orangeville road is now but a dirt trail that leads down the side of a gully. In pioneer times, buggies and wagons laden with grain strained up the steep road.

In the lilac bushes lining the path lurk a lonely cabin and several foundations, including those of a black-smith shop, a church, the Orange Lodge, several cabins and the Beamish Hotel. The only structure still standing on what was formerly the main street is the cabin now known as the Pettit House. It remains privately owned.

When a proposed golf course resort complex threatened the tiny village in the 1990s, the remaining residents rallied to fight the proposal at the Ontario Municipal Board. To help raise the money to cover their legal costs, residents dressed in period costumes and, for a few years, hosted "ghost town" walks, leading visitors to the now ghostly building sites of this once-busy community.

Ballycroy lies on the Ballycroy Road about a kilometre (half a mile) northwest of the intersection of Highways 9 and 50.

Ballycroy's false-fronted former store
marks an early pioneer intersection
that once boasted three hotels.

The former miller's house still
stands in Boston Mills along with
a lone workers' cabin.

BOSTON MILLS

By the 1820s the banks of the Credit River were lined with dozens of fledgling mill villages, among them one that would become Boston Mills. As settlement progressed, Alexander Dick in 1850 built a dam for a carding and sawmill. After he sold it to Hiram Caslor, the place became known as Caslor's Corners.

Its more popular name, however, originated with the rowdy Saturday night dances held in nearby Cheltenham. After the final notes of the popular reel "The Road to Boston" faded into the dawn, partiers would stagger past the mill on their way home. Caslor painted the name "Boston" on the side of his mill, and the name stuck. Later on, even the CPR called its local flag station "Boston."

In 1860 Caslor added a gristmill, which by 1880 had incorporated a more modern roller system. Area residents used a hall located above the mill as a community centre. The final owner of the mill was Henry Bracken. In addition to the mill, Boston Mills also contained a hotel, a school, a post office, a store, a butchery, and, in connection with the gristmill, a distillery. A number of workers' homes lined the sides of the river.

When the Hamilton & Northwestern and CPR railways were built, they located small stations to serve the village, although neither was close enough to significantly affect its development. The HNW depot, with a grain elevator beside it, lay on the 32nd Side Road connected to the village by a boardwalk, while that of the CPR stood on the 2nd Line.

In 1910 fire destroyed Bracken's mill and several nearby buildings. None were rebuilt; however, a small power plant was built on the old mill site and lasted until 1931, when a flood washed it away.

The ravages of Hurricane Hazel in 1954 left little evidence of the mills other than vague foundations upstream from the bridge. However, the mill owner's house still stands, a two-storey frame structure situated a short distance north of the intersection. Behind it, although not visible from the road, a surviving mill worker's cabin is said to be among the oldest structures in the region, while a short distance east of the bridge, another early village home survives. A few newer homes, and another early home, stand south of Boston Mills Road.

On the northwest corner of the intersection sprawls Boston Mills' most prominent landmark, the extensive cemetery. The first burial date in the cemetery is 1823, that of David Williams who was, according to a plaque, buried "in the bark of the tree that killed him." The stone schoolhouse, SS #8 built in 1888, now functions as a chapel for interments.

The village lies at the intersection of Boston Mills Road and Chingacousy Road, northeast of the picturesque village of Cheltenham.

The gaunt shells of the Cheltenham
kilns have been preserved by the
current clay extractors.

CHELTENHAM BRICK WORKS

The gaunt shells of the Cheltenham Brick Works have long been landscape icons on Mississauga Road a short distance west of the hamlet of Cheltenham. Looming high over a weedy field, they are probably the most impressive ruins in the GTA.

Beneath the limestone layers of the Niagara Escarpment lies a deposit of Medina Shale. A hard red clay, the deposit proved to be superb for brick making, and the many outcroppings in the Niagara Escarpment area gave rise to several brick-making operations. Such brickworks started up around Milton, and, in Terra Cotta, produced an industry that gave the village its name (it had previously gone by the name of Salmonville). One of the largest outcroppings of the shale occurred about 2 km (1.2 miles) west of Cheltenham.

In 1914 the Interprovincial Brick Company acquired the site and began to turn out bricks, 90,000 at a time. The operation consisted of six downdraft kilns and one continuously burning kiln. Although some workers lived in nearby Cheltenham, others preferred to live in one of the 14 houses that the company built on the site, paying rent of just $13 a month. Once manufactured, the bricks were shipped out from a siding on the CN railway immediately adjacent to the site.

By the 1950s Cheltenham itself was on the verge of becoming a ghost town. Its mills, industries and hotels had all closed; only the store remained open. Had it not been for the brickworks, Cheltenham would have died.

Then, in 1958, Domtar bought the brickworks and shut them down. Although they demolished the houses, the kilns survived. Later, another company, Brampton Brick, purchased the property and proposed to demolish the aging landmarks to excavate more clay. Because the site lay within the Niagara Escarpment Planning Area, permission to excavate required public hearings. Some groups wanted a wildlife preserve, others a historical designation, while Brampton Brick pushed for an exemption to allow the excavation. Ultimately a compromise was reached. After agreeing to stabilize and preserve the shells of the historic kilns, Brampton Brick got its permission.

Today, the clay piles lie high behind the ruins, all protected by a chain link fence. Inside the fence the company has helpfully placed a sketch that depicts the historic brickworks and the workers' village as they appeared at their peak around 1930.

The photogenic kilns and chimneys are located on Mississauga Road north of King St. and northwest of Brampton. North of the kilns is the new excavation site, while still further north, and south of the kilns, shrubs cover the sites of the houses. The route of the historic railway is now the Caledon Rail Trail, which offers a small parking area for trail users.

The Darnley gristmill is a ghostly
reminder of Crooks Hollow's days
as a busy industrial centre.

CROOKS HOLLOW

Above Spencer Creek on the Crooks Hollow Road near Dundas looms a crumbling stone shell. Built in 1813, it is considered to be one of Ontario's oldest ruins and is just one of the remains of the early industrial empire of James Crooks and of the community which became Crooks Hollow.

In the valley carved out by the waters of Spencer Creek, Crooks, an early entrepreneur, established a sprawling industrial complex. By 1829 he had added to the gristmill a distillery, a linseed oil mill, a cooperage, a card clothing factory, a fulling and drying works, a tannery, a woollen mill, a foundry, an agricultural implement factory and Upper Canada's first paper mill. The settlement also included a general store and inn, while the families of Crooks' 100-man work force lived in cabins and houses that lined the narrow valley road.

The industries thrived for more than half a century. But the railways bypassed the community in favour of Dundas, and many Crooks Hollow industries relocated to trackside, although some of its mills and factories survived into the twentieth century. The stone gristmill, then known as the Darnley Mill, lasted until 1934 when it burned, leaving only the stone walls.

Most of the former townsite lies along the Crooks Hollow Road east and west of the mill. Village homes sat on the south side of the road west of the bridge over the river on sites today occupied by newer houses. East of the bridge, a string of log cabins that housed mill workers lined the south side of the road, again, a site now occupied by modern homes.

On the north side of the road, an old home sits away from the roadside; it was the residence of James Stutt who had purchased the mill from Crooks. A short distance further east, again on the north side, another older private house marks the home built by James Morden for his father, Jonathan. Father and son had constructed grist- and sawmills on the river on the south side of the road. These mills burned in 1905, and all vestiges of the mill and its dam have long since vanished.

The most prominent ruins, however, remain those of the Darnley gristmill. After it was sold to Stutt in 1860, it was converted into a paper mill and operated until it was gutted by fire in 1934. The walls, massive and photogenic, loom beside the road, and, although fenced off, can be easily photographed from the road. Much of the valley is owned by the Hamilton Region Conservation Authority, which has published a site guide to the ghost town of Crooks Hollow.

GREENLAW CORNERS

As urban sprawl engulfs the farmland and the rural routes across the Greater Toronto Area, it becomes increasingly difficult to identify the early pioneer hamlets so necessary to the first settlers. Many have disappeared with little trace. Greenlaw Corners was one.

In 1938 the *Toronto Telegram* published an article entitled "Lone Crumbling Church Only Remaining Symbol of Onetime Busy Hamlet." "The passing of years has brought many changes to hamlets throughout Ontario," the piece continued. "Many have blossomed into industrial towns, many have passed into oblivion, remembered only by the old-timers." According to the article, Greenlaw at one time included a furniture factory, a church, a wagon shop, a blacksmith shop, homes and a population of 400. "Few today remember Greenlaw," the piece concluded, "and the ranks of those who do are being slowly depleted by the Grim Reaper."

An early map, published in 1859, showed a cabinetmaker, a dulcimer maker and a Union church. A later map, from 1877, showed a cemetery and parsonage as well. The original church was closed around 1900 and the congregation moved to the Melville church, a short distance to the south.

Greenlaw Corners was described as being "picturesquely" situated on the Fifth Sideroad of Caledon Township, at the Fourth Line about "two miles," (3 km), from Belfountain. Its sole survivor then was, as the headline noted, a "crumbling" church, and the cemetery.

The "crumbling" church has gone now, but its heir, the white wooden Melville Church, still survives. Built in 1837, it is one of Ontario's oldest wooden churches. Nearby is the former school, a handsome stone building now a private home. Most of Greenlaw's structures clustered about the northwest corner of the Grange Road and what is today Mississauga Road, but the only vestige there now is the small cemetery where the gravestones have been gathered together in a common cement frame. A small cabin, much modernized, is also an early survivor.

On both the Grange Road and Mississauga Road, close to their intersection, heritage plaques proclaim "Greenlaw, established in the 1870s as a pioneer Baptist community knows as The Grange. it declined in the 1920s."

The 4th Line now goes by the more familiar name of Mississauga Road. The church and school are located about a kilometre (half a mile) north of Old Base Line Road or 4 km (2.5 miles) south of Belfountain. The church is on the west side; the school on the east a short distance north of the church. The Grange Road is a short distance further north.

One of Ontario's oldest surviving wooden churches, Melville Church, served the now-vanished settlement of Greenlaw Corners.

A stone boarding house and hotel is the only
evidence of the early village that provided
homes and businesses at Guelph Junction.

GUELPH JUNCTION

As early as 1857 the city of Guelph had enjoyed a Grand Trunk Railway connection to the port of Toronto and the terminus at Sarnia. However, when the Credit Valley Railway was completed, linking Streetsville Junction on the Canadian Pacific Railway's main line with St. Thomas, a busy railway town in southwestern Ontario, it passed well to the south of Guelph.

Anxious to reduce their shipping costs through competition, the citizens of Guelph in 1888 incorporated the Guelph Junction Railway. The short line provided them with their much-desired link with the Grand Trunk's rival, Canadian Pacific. From the junction, a link with the city of Hamilton was added in 1912 and a busy railway village grew up at this point. In addition to the sprawling single-storey station, there were sorting yards, a water tank and coaling dock, as well as homes and boarding houses for the train crews.

The village portion of the town lined the tracks on the south side of the yard. When the route was extended west from Guelph to Goderich on Lake Huron in 1907, the line became known as the Guelph & Goderich Railway. Traffic increased and the junction village grew.

A little over a century later, however, the line from Guelph to Goderich was lifted. A decade after that, the 20 km (12.5 mile) track from Guelph to Guelph Junction was turned over to the city of Guelph. Although traffic from Lake Huron no longer calls, the location remains busy as trains bring freight from the industries in Guelph to the main line. The yards also store GO trains, which run from Milton to Toronto.

With the removal of most of the other yard functions and the opening of roads to the site, train crews no longer needed the accommodation that Guelph Junction had provided, and many of the early buildings have been removed. Sadly, among them was the historic station. While a few newer homes have been built around the village, the only survivor of its days as a busy railway junction is the old stone boarding house/hotel.

Guelph Junction lies at the end of Guelph Junction Road just north of the Campbellville Road.

JOSEPHINE

The most rewarding ghost towns are those that come at the end of a hike, far from the nearest road. And Josephine, although small with scant remains, fits that category.

This was a sawmill village that began shortly after the North Simcoe Railway laid its tracks through the timber-rich Minesing Swamp northwest of modern-day Barrie. Here, in 1879, Joseph Budd built a sawmill to cut the cedar, alder, birch, maple and spruce that grew thick in the wetland. For nearly four decades the mill turned out shingles and staves. When Budd succeeded in acquiring a post office, he named it after his daughter.

As there was no other community nearby, Budd built his own, providing housing for his workers as well as a company store, post office and classroom. The post office in fact also served as both school and church. The site had a railway flag stop for travellers heading for Allandale or Penetanguishene, although it is unknown if a station building was ever actually constructed.

A devastating fire destroyed most of the village in 1885, but Budd quickly rebuilt. He could not, however, survive the loss of the swamp's stands of timber, and the mill finally closed in 1914.

As the village site remained well away from any public road, the remains of Budd's house and his workers' village simply crumbled silently into ruin. Today the rails are gone, but the route of this ghost railway now forms a link on the North Simcoe Railtrail.

The site of Josephine lies along the trail halfway between George Johnson Road and Vespra Valley Road, about 8 km (5 miles) west of Barrie. Here, the stone foundation of Budd's house can be seen to the north of the trail, along with the collapsing shells of a shed and barn. On the south side of the trail, where the mill was located, an overgrown meadow contains a wooden shell and the vague cellar holes of the workers' village.

Near the site of the flag stop, a stucco-covered outhouse, which still survives, was likely for the use of those awaiting the arrival of the weekly train. Here, too, beside a bench for weary walkers, a historical plaque outlines the history of the remote little ghost town.

Another ghost heritage site lies west of George Johnson Road. Here, the conservation authority has reconstructed the palisade of Fort Willow, or Willow Creek Depot, which served as a British supply garrison during the war of 1812.

Several old structures mark the location of the home of Josephine's mill owner, Joseph Budd.

A collapsing shell is the sole
survivor of the mill workers'
cabins in Josephine.

The original Patterson family home still
stands and is honoured as one of the
grandest heritage homes in the otherwise
bleak Richmond Hill area.

PATTERSON

Peter Patterson and his brothers were early settlers who had followed Yonge Street 25 km (15 miles) north from tiny York to their farm plot west of what is now Richmond Hill. Starting with a sawmill, they expanded into the manufacture of farm implements. The company also refined an innovative process for tempering steel, a technology they sold to other manufacturers.

As the enterprise grew, the Pattersons added acommodation for their workers. The village they created included boarding houses and 25 single houses for families. The only store, however, was that operated by the company itself. The post office, which was located in the store, took the name of the community's founding family.

By 1871 the population of Patterson had reached 500. The workforce of 200 included 23 machinists, 17 carpenters, 21 labourers, 8 blacksmiths, 10 moulders and four painters.

After the railways had made their way into the area, the company lobbied the local municipality to finance a spur line to the operation. The municipality balked, however, and in 1885 the town of Woodstock offered the Pattersons $35,000 to relocate to their town, where they could enjoy rail access. Within two years, the company had gone, leaving the village abandoned.

Although the site seems ready to fall victim to the GTA's relentless sprawl, a number of vestiges yet remain. On Major MacKenzie Road, a busy suburban road, three of the company homes still stand on the north side of the road. All three are identical, stand close together and represent the last of the 25 houses that the Pattersons had built. The site is identified by a historical plaque (although stopping to read it on the heavily travelled road could be risky). A large barn-like building of buff-coloured brick further west is the factory where farm implements were made, while the white house to its east is the former boarding house.

West of the factory stands one the area's most attractive early houses, the home of the Pattersons themselves. With its delicate gingerbread work and its shady grounds, it will soon be a delightful anomaly in Richmond Hill's expanding urban wasteland.

This painting shows the layout of the factory town of Patterson before the owners moved their operations to Woodstock in the 1870s.

Concrete bridge abutments mark
the site of the original road and mill
dam in the little ghost settlement of
Sinclairville.

Sinclairville's original main street is
now a grassy lawn beside the ghost
village's only surviving home.

SINCLAIRVILLE

From simple beginnings as a mill site on the waters of Chippewa Creek, Sinclairville grew into a thriving pioneer community. Here, the Baron family operated a water-powered sawmill, while Robert Hewitt added a steam sawmill and a shingle mill. The Hewitt family, with John, James and Robert, became the village's most prominent entrepreneurs, operating the mills, blacksmith shop and carpentry shop.

South of the mills, the streets of Sinclairville also contained a pair of stores, two blacksmith shops and two hotels, the Crawford House and Wilson Hotel. One of the blacksmiths, John Hewitt, manufactured dental forceps, which he used for his secondary occupation, dentistry. A short distance south of the village stood the original frame church, which served Anglican, Methodist and Presbyterian worshippers alike. It was replaced in 1908 by the present brick church.

Most of the early village buildings were clustered around the T intersection at the end of James Street. Here, just north of the church, were the Fred Mitchell house, Wilson's store and hotel, and the barn and ice house for the hotel (all on the north side of the road). Opposite them was John Robinson's shoe-making emporium.

Around the corner were Robinson's rug-making shop and Hewitt's blacksmith shop, beside which stood two of the Hewitt family homes. To the north of the homes were John Hewitt's carpentry shop and Robert Crawford's hotel. To the east of James Street and behind the store were the shingle mill and Robert Hewitt's steam sawmill. From here, James Street angled east to cross Chippewa Creek, where it passed Robert Hewitt's large home. By 1948, however, the little village could claim only four houses, the church and a chopping mill. Today, of these buildings, only the James and Robert Hewitt homes still stand.

The village remained modest in size, and when the railways bypassed it both to the north (the Great Western) and to the south (the Canada Southern), its fate as a quiet country hamlet was sealed. Although the flow of water in the creek was steady, more than water was needed to power the new industries that the railway era ushered in. As the services that Sinclairville offered became redundant, the smithies, the hotels and the stores closed and Sinclairville became a ghost town. Now, residents from surrounding areas hold ghost walks in its wake.

An improved and straightened new road angles across the former village streets, wiping away several of the old lots and foundations. South of the new bridge, the original main street has become a residential laneway with just one original structure still on it. North of the bridge, where the mills once stood, the original road alignment can be discerned in the gully beside the road, with another original village structure nearby.

Follow Highway 20 south from Hamilton to Empire Corners and then take Road 9 east to the gravelled Sinclairville Road. Turn left here and travel a short distance to the brick church and the old townsite beyond that.

Pickerel Landing's CPR station was the village's
main shipping point and resembled most of the
stations along the railway's Sudbury line.

INDEX